PRAISE FOR *PREP FOR SUCCESS*

• • • • • • • • • • • • • • •

"This book shares the story of Paul and Steve's success. After you read their book, the sequel will be yours to write!"

—DAVID NOUR

Bestselling Author, Relationship Economics *and* Co-Create

"An outstanding and motivating read for all aspiring entrepreneurs who are trapped inside an employee's body!"

—CATHERINE MONSON

Vice Chair, International Franchise Association (IFA)
CEO and President, FASTSIGNS International, Inc.

"Paul and Steve's journey to success echoes that of my own. This is a fantastic read for anyone who ever thought about starting their own business!"

—REGGIE AGGARWAL

Founder and CEO, Cvent

"As valued members of the franchise community, Paul and Steve bring important insights to prospective business owners."

—ROBERT CRESANTI

President and CEO, International Franchise Association

"This book will inspire you to fire your boss!"

—KELLY PERDEW

Founder and General Partner, Moonshots Capital

Winner, The Apprentice *(Season 2)*

"I loved Prep for Success *and especially loved the stories of Paul and Steve. The reader will clearly see that Paul and Steve have high levels of character, chemistry, care, and competence. Those are four qualities I would want to see in any business partner. That, plus their record of success, makes* Prep for Success *a must read for anyone at a crossroad in their life who is looking for an entrepreneurial opportunity."*

—GORDON J. BERNHARDT

President and CEO, Bernhardt Wealth Management, Inc.

PREP *~ for ~* SUCCESS

PREP ~ for ~ SUCCESS

The Entrepreneur's Guide to
Achieving Your Dreams

STEVE DAVIS & PAUL TRAPP

Advantage

Published by Advantage, Charleston, South Carolina
Member of Advantage Media Group

ADVANTAGE is a registered trademark, and the Advantage colophon is a trademark of Advantage Media Group, Inc.

Printed in the United States of America

10 9 8 7 6 5 4 3 2 1

ISBN: 978-1-64225-051-0
LCCN: 2019908459

Book design by Jamie Wise

This publication is designed to provide accurate and authoritative information in regard to the subject matter covered. It is sold with the understanding that the publisher is not engaged in rendering legal, accounting, or other professional services. If legal advice or other expert assistance is required, the services of a competent professional person should be sought.

Advantage Media Group is proud to be a part of the Tree Neutral® program. Tree Neutral offsets the number of trees consumed in the production and printing of this book by taking proactive steps such as planting trees in direct proportion to the number of trees used to print books. To learn more about Tree Neutral, please visit **www.treeneutral.com**.

TreeNeutral

Advantage Media Group is a publisher of business, self-improvement, and professional development books and online learning. We help entrepreneurs, business leaders, and professionals share their Stories, Passion, and Knowledge to help others Learn & Grow. Do you have a manuscript or book idea that you would like us to consider for publishing? Please visit **advantagefamily.com** or call **1.866.775.1696**.

This book is dedicated to the many men and women in our lives who believed in us, encouraged us, mentored us, and prepared us our entire lives for this very moment. We pray this book serves as a humble return on your investment.

TABLE OF CONTENTS
• • • • • • • • • • • •

THE UNPLANNED EVENT

ARE YOU READY?

PREP FOR SUCCESS

RECOGNIZING OPPORTUNITY

BECOMING A DISRUPTOR

ATTRACTING TALENT

ESTABLISHING A CULTURE

BEFRIENDING MURPHY

FOREWORD

· · · · · · · · · · · · · ·

As a note of background, I'm a serial entrepreneur, having built six companies in my earlier years, and for the past couple decades have been traveling the world coaching others on how to do the same. I can remember first meeting Paul and Steve as if it were just yesterday, even though it now marks more than a decade ago. I was in Washington, DC, delivering a three-hour session to a relatively small group of thirty CEOs at a Vistage meeting, and sitting in the back in full army uniforms, there they were. As a former captain in the army dating back to the early '70s, I knew there had to be a good reason for them to be there, but I sure couldn't figure it out!

Once my session ended, they introduced themselves and indicated that they would soon be exiting the military and were in the process of launching an event planning company and wanted to assess my fit as a speaker for their audience of military recruiters. They were exuberant as to the fit and we soon agreed for my first of many speaking engagements with Federal Conference.

It wasn't long before I determined that these guys were serious operators, and they were "all in" as to building the foundations of success for their budding business:

1. Vision—it was big, and they owned it.

2. Commitment—to do things right.

3. Culture—lead with the heart, and make it family-like.

It was as if they read my book on how to build a successful business, but I hadn't written it yet (*Hyper Sales Growth* was published in 2014). My greatest frustration as a professional speaker is knowing how well my teachings work and how so few take action. I warn my audiences to not let it "die in the room," and clearly these guys weren't going to do that! They say it best in their book: "Every single event in life is a Super Bowl if you really want to be successful."

As I read their book prior to writing this foreword, it was gratifying to see so many of my teachings put into action in their personal style; for example:

1. The importance of systems and processes, regularly updated with new learnings and maintained in a firm-wide playbook. I love this line from their book: "After all, killing the elephant is the easy part … getting it out of the jungle is where it gets tricky."

2. Trust is the bedrock of all that is successful, encompassing actions inside and outside the company.

3. Business and growth are driven by relationships, which are cultivated best by regularly adding value along the way.

4. Perception of value is critical to differentiating from all others.

5. Designing your uniqueness will separate you from all others.

The list goes on and it's all in this book!

Steve and Paul have done a superb job of researching the market they chose to enter and have identified its growth opportunities. When you commit to building a business based on the principles they so fervently believe in, and grabbing a share of market of even 1

STEVE DAVIS & PAUL TRAPP

percent positions you as a market leader, my words of advice for all involved are "hang on for a fun and profitable ride."

Paul sure took those early words of advice from his two-star general to heart: "Go find people of promise and enable them to become."

—JACK DALY

CEO, Entrepreneur, Bestselling Author, Business Coach, and Endurance Athlete www.jackdalysales.com

ACKNOWLEDGMENTS

• • • • • • • • • • • • • •

As best friends, business partners, and now coauthors, we are writing this book to share our collective journey and business insight with the readers. Our story is transitional in nature and focuses on the importance of preperation and preparing for success. When we think about the countless people that have provided us with what we needed to write this book, so many names come to mind of family, friends, teachers, mentors, past leaders, employees, franchisees, and clients alike. We are so very grateful to each of you for touching our lives, the experiences we've shared, the love we've felt, and the wisdom we've been blessed with, all just from knowing you. While some of you are mentioned by name in this book, all of you will remain in our hearts forever.

As individuals, we also have our own stories, experiences, and relationships that warrant some special recognition as well. Please indulge us for a moment while we each acknowledge a few special people from our hearts.

From Paul's heart—I can't imagine where I'd be without God's presence in my life and the positive influence each of you has had on me. To Ellen Barol, my high school English teacher and the first adult beside my parents who ever saw good in me. To the mentors who challenged me, cheered me on, and fueled my growth—LTC (Ret) Bob Lewis, COL (Ret) Rich Guzzetta, Pat Higgs, and Jack Daly—I carry each of you close in my heart wherever I go. To our early business partners, Cynthia Dehner and Corey Holeman, thank you for helping us shape and mold the foundation of our success.

To my mother, Sally, who loved me unconditionally and encouraged and inspired my entrepreneurial spirit from a very young age. To my best friend and coauthor, Steve, for always putting our friendship first, and accepting me despite my flaws. To my three adult children, Brendan, Paul, and Emma, the three of you are my heart. And finally, to the woman who literally changed my life forever, my wife, Kimberly ... It's because of you I wake up every morning trying to be a better man, husband, and father.

From Steve's heart—I would like to thank my parents, Jack and Lucille Davis, both so very strong in their own right. My father, a prisoner of war survivor, taught me to do what I promise, that a man's word is his bond, and that the true meaning behind a handshake is reputation and integrity. My mother bore six children and, after my father's passing, raised three of us on her own. My mother, a saint to me, attended church daily and was my constant moral and spiritual compass.

I would also like to acknowledge Mark Klayman. We worked together as cops. I quickly realized he was very disciplined, much like my father. Although he became my supervisor, I considered him a mentor and friend. Mark taught me that doing the right thing is not always easy or popular, that a hard, righteous decision is better than an easy, bad one. Mark went on to become the chief of police at our department.

For me, Jack Daly solidifies the attributes of success in business. He helped Paul and me understand that to be successful, we must first be prepared, which takes focus and dedication to those around you. Thank you, Jack; "Onward and Upward," my friend.

Paul Trapp is my best friend, business partner, and the coauthor of this book. I am so thankful for you, your love, and our relationship. I don't know where I'd be today if we hadn't met. I only know that I am a better man for knowing you. I love you like a brother, because that's what you are, my brother in Christ.

Thank you to my wife, Jessica, and daughter, Maggie: without your love and support throughout my journey, I would have nothing to write about. You are my everything and I love you both dearly.

Ultimately, we (Paul and Steve) are the authors of this book, but we can't take all the credit for our success. You see, it was our employees, past and present, that truly built these companies into the successful entities they are today. It is their talent, their problem-solving skills, their innovation and passion that earned our place in the industry. We were simply blessed to provide vision and watch them grow.

Of the many rock star employees we've hired and worked with over the years, we'd both be remiss if we didn't recognize five senior leaders that continued to support us even during our toughest times. The Fab-Five: Denise Radcliff, Kelly McWhinney, Femi Shodeinde, Jessica Davis, and Tina Mincks. We will forever be indebted to you for trusting our vision and the many sacrifices you made to share in our mutual success.

In closing, we'd like to thank you, the reader, for including us as a small part of your personal journey. We hope the investment of time you make to read *Prep for Success: The Entrepreneur's Guide to Achieving Your Dreams* helps you to recognize that you've been preparing your entire life for this very moment, and you too are prepped for success!

THE UNPLANNED EVENT

• •

Give me six hours to chop down a tree and I will
spend the first four sharpening the axe.

—ABRAHAM LINCOLN

Not everything in life goes as planned. In some instances, a single unplanned event could change the trajectory of your life in an instant. We've all heard about the "lucky" guy who wins the lottery, only to find years later that his life is in complete shambles with a broken family, a mountain of debt, and nothing to show for his "good" fortune. Was he prepared?

Success isn't traditionally tied to a single life event like winning the lottery, but rather to a series of planned and unplanned life events that ultimately deliver you success. This book won't tell you what success looks like, as success lies in the eyes of the beholder. What this book will do is help you to prepare for the day when success—or any opportunity—shows up on your doorstep, announced or unannounced.

In 2013, success didn't just knock on the doors of Paul Trapp and Steve Davis; it kicked their doors in like federal agents executing a no-knock search warrant. It was the same year *The Wolf of Wall Street* hit the theaters. At one point in the movie, Leonardo DiCaprio's character says: "The year I turned twenty-six, as the head of my own brokerage firm, I made $49 million … which really pissed me off, because it was three shy of a million a week."

> IN 2013, SUCCESS DIDN'T JUST KNOCK ON THE DOORS OF PAUL TRAPP AND STEVE DAVIS; IT KICKED THEIR DOORS IN LIKE FEDERAL AGENTS EXECUTING A NO-KNOCK SEARCH WARRANT.

Ironically, that's exactly how much Paul and Steve achieved in sales in 2013—just under a million dollars a week. That's where the similarities to the movie end, though. They weren't necessarily "pissed" that their business, Federal Conference (FederalConference.com), had reached such a level of success—they felt blessed. And more importantly, their revenue was legit … and nobody went to jail! After all, they weren't the wolves of Wall Street. They were more like … Fred and Barney from the old *Flintstones* cartoons. Fred was the louder, larger, more boisterous character, always coming up with some harebrained scheme, while Barney was the skeptical, kindhearted, loyal companion who went along with Fred and hoped for the best.

That's essentially Paul and Steve, respectively: the Fred and Barney of event planning, but equipped with some no-nonsense, world-class military training. While they've been business partners for years, let's rewind to the beginning, when they first met and became friends.

A FUNNY THING HAPPENED ON THE WAY TO THE SEMINARY

The night Paul and Steve met was the ultimate unplanned event. Paul was working as a temporary manager for a very large nightclub in Central Florida at the time—definitely not his calling in life, but it's where his particular journey had led him at that point. He was home from the army, a young lieutenant fresh out of Officer Candidate School. Everything seemed to be going well. Paul had only been back for a few days when the owner of the club approached him with an employment offer. She apparently had just fired her nightclub manager, and not being a night owl herself, needed someone she could trust to temporarily fill the role and lock up every night while she figured out a more permanent solution.

At that point in his life, however, Paul was a few short months away from attending St. Meinrad Seminary and School of Theology in Indiana. He wanted to be a Catholic priest, not a nightclub manager. But with time on his hands, he accepted the position. Basically, he was simply there to inventory the liquor, schedule the staff, count the money, and put the key in the door at the end of the night. The club could hold five hundred people, and there were only a few nights a week that it would fill to capacity.

On one of the busiest nights, someone pulled a gun out and shot it off in the air. The shooter didn't aim for anyone in particular, just fired.

If you've never witnessed five hundred people scramble all at once through one or two exits, it is quite a sight. The staff called 911 and the police responded. The staff didn't know if someone had been shot. Fortunately there wasn't any blood on the dance floor. The police were checking with the hospitals and trying to figure out if someone had been shot or not, looking around for signs of damage. Before long, the police supervisor for the shift came by to check on his officers. That supervisor was Steve Davis.

When Steve arrived on the scene, one of his officers approached him outside and reported that everything was under control. It appeared no one had been shot; it most likely had been someone fooling around and discharging a weapon. Then the officer said to Steve, "I want you to come inside and meet this new nightclub manager. He's going to be a Catholic priest."

Steve was and still is very much devoted to his faith, which is Catholicism. There were several occasions while serving on the SWAT team that he was asked to pray for the safety of the team before they kicked in the doors while serving a search warrant.

"I don't know if this nightclub manager is going to be a Catholic priest," Steve replied. "I'll be the judge of that." So he went in to size Paul up. That's the night they first met, and eventually the two became friends. With Steve working midnight shift, he'd stop by the nightclub, just to walk through and check in on Paul to make sure he was okay. They would talk for ten or fifteen minutes, then Steve would go off and do his thing. Then one day Steve invited Paul to breakfast after work. The two men really hit it off. As a matter of fact, Steve was with Paul the day Paul met his wife, Kimberly.

The two friends were in the nightclub when a beautiful young lady started talking with them. Paul was smitten. She ended up talking to both guys, but she was initially attracted to Steve. She really liked him, but Paul really liked her. Paul thought to himself, "This is not going to work. This is not the way things are supposed to happen." But he was on the way to seminary anyway, so he figured everything was going according to God's plan. After all, Paul was supposed to go serve God. Catholic priests don't get married, don't have kids. But he was *really* attracted to her.

Mind you, this was at a time when the world didn't have cell phones, only pagers. Kimberly got Steve's pager number, and she says she paged him, but for some reason he never received it. God's plan? Paul thinks so! So the three of them continued chatting every once in a while. Before long, Kimberly and Paul started dating. He was still a National Guard officer, and as August approached, he started thinking about winding down and gearing up for seminary. Steve was still a cop at that point, and the guys were still buddying around. Then on August 24, 1992, Hurricane Andrew hit South Florida and caused total devastation.

Paul was mobilized as a National Guard officer, and Steve was mobilized as a cop to help the South Florida police forces during their time of need, and stay there until the community returned to normalcy. During that time, being away from his job as a nightclub manager, from Kimberly, and from the concept of seminary, Paul had a lot of time to work hard and serve the community. But he was also thinking about Kimberly.

When it was all said and done, Paul came back from deployment and found that he had missed his start date for seminary. His vocations director told Paul he would reschedule him for another semester, so suddenly Paul had more time on his hands. Sure enough, in that short time, his love for Kimberly just grew stronger and stronger, and his desire to go off to seminary became weaker and weaker. He never set foot in the seminary. Unplanned events changed Paul's trajectory before he ever got there.

DAYDREAMING OF MORE

By that time, the nightclub owner had already hired a permanent manager, so Paul was now a thirty-year-old, unemployed, part-time National Guard officer, living at home with his parents. He thought about going back on active duty, but at that time they weren't accepting reserve officers. So one day Steve said, "Hey, we're hiring at the police department." Paul thought to himself, *Okay. I used to be in the military police. I could do that.* He was pretty excited about that option because he had gone riding with Steve a few times and really liked what his new friend did for a living.

So Paul became a cop. Then, Paul recruited Steve to the National Guard. That's when everything came together. They weren't business owners yet, just friends and cops. Paul was the best man in Steve's wedding. Steve was the best man in Paul's wedding. The two became intimately involved in each other's families. They vacationed together. They served as cops together. They served as soldiers together. They deployed together. They deployed separately. They took care of each other's families while the other was deployed. They are the de facto godfather of each other's kids. Paul carried Steve's mom's casket to the grave and Steve carried Paul's mom's casket to the grave. You just don't get closer in life by choice.

The folks who knew them lovingly referred to them as *The Steve and Paul Show.* They were both stars of their own little weekly sitcom, which was their lives. They would hang out in the garage and drink beer. Or stand around the barbecue pit just talking and dreaming. They dreamed about so many things. Steve kept saying, "I just think we should invent something. Look at these people inventing technology, or platforms like Facebook ... and they're rich! We just have to figure out *what* to invent."

Paul and Steve both had long been daydreamers. They always seemed to be distracted, dreaming, scheming, looking at the world through a different lens, from an entrepreneurial perspective of taking the lead and controlling their own destinies. Even if neither one could articulate or put a name to what they felt, they knew they were different. The fact is, however, that most schools in the Western world aren't exactly geared toward teaching future entrepreneurs ... they're teaching future *employees*.

Most of us are trained from a very early age to know the system we need to adhere to: a good education leads to a good job, which leads to a career with benefits and advancement opportunities, which leads to climbing the corporate ladder until retirement. Most people reading this can relate to this scenario. Usually our first jobs are not likely to be something we're particularly passionate about, just something to pay the bills. But when we start maturing and looking toward the future, we often pick a job or a career field that seems interesting and relatively rewarding. That passion launches a career, and at first it's enough. A teacher, for example, takes great pride in connecting with students and enlightening young minds on their educational journeys. In the years that follow some of them become teacher of the year, then vice principal, then perhaps principal. Eventually they are named the superintendent of the district, continuing to put more distance between them and what it was they loved to do, which was teach.

With each step up the career ladder, you separate yourself further from your passion. And with each one of those milestones comes a pay raise and a new lifestyle—the bigger mortgage, the nicer car, the private school for the kids.

And then one day you wake up and realize you've been caught in a cycle within a closed system, with limited opportunities to realize your real dreams ... the ones you still daydream about. That's exactly what happened to Paul and Steve while in their respective careers, sitting around the grill on the weekends, dreaming of what could be. They had elevated themselves and excelled in their jobs. They had earned the promotions and made as much money as they could possibly make while working for someone else. They went as high as they could go ... and then they reached that tipping point. It was time for them to stop making someone else rich and start working for themselves.

PREP FOR SUCCESS

So they started one business, then another. They started a not-for-profit that helped kids with after-school programs. The pair just did things that sounded right at the time. For them, those were all the practice runs or false starts for what they are doing today. Those years were all leading up to building something bigger—the once (or twice!) in a lifetime, hit-the-jackpot, Mega Millions lottery moment: Federal Conference and EventPrep.

Federal Conference combines several decades of successful event planning experience in both the private and government sectors. It currently manages hundreds of millions of dollars in government and commercial contracts. Its team of sixty-plus meeting professionals plans and executes more than three thousand events annually. The success of this company, as well as its experience in military, positioned Paul and Steve for their next venture.

EventPrep, a home-based, lifestyle franchise opportunity, is a forward-thinking, full-service event planning and management company headquartered in Central Florida. It leverages Federal Conference's globally recognized brand name while capitalizing on Paul and Steve's in-depth industry experience and relationships. EventPrep has a global reach, and its primary focus is to save clients time, money, and anxiety while planning unforgettable events.

Paul and Steve didn't plan to capture the number-one spot in a $25 billion industry. They didn't plan to eventually go on to have hundreds of millions of dollars in contracts. Nor did they plan to experience nearly 25,000 percent growth over the first three years and make the Inc. 500 twice, ranked number twenty-three and number two—becoming the second fastest growing privately held company in the US.

They may not have planned for this level of success, but Paul and Steve were certainly prepared. Why? Success doesn't happen because you plan for it. Success is a result of being *prepared* for it. As the saying goes, trophies are earned on the practice field and picked up at tournaments. Success in anything is a result of grueling preparation, whether you're a Super Bowl quarterback or a concert musician who

SUCCESS DOESN'T HAPPEN BECAUSE YOU PLAN FOR IT. SUCCESS IS A RESULT OF BEING *PREPARED* FOR IT.

performs at Carnegie Hall. It's in the drudgery, the daily grind, the routine practicing, the endless drills that eventually transform learning into experience and experience into instinct.

Paul and Steve may be preparation experts, but you're no stranger to it. Preparation is ingrained in our day-to-day lives, in the things we do without thinking. What you are having for dinner tonight is a result of preparation, or a maybe a lack thereof. But whether it's a five-course meal, leftovers, or carryout, you are prepared to eat something. The trips you take, the clean clothes you wear, the job you have, the car you drive all are a result of a certain degree of preparation. If you live in Florida, you prepare for hurricanes. If you live in New England, you prepare for snow. If you live in California, you prepare for earthquakes.

Preparation, you see, is everywhere. And whatever your current career choice, wherever you are personally or professionally in life, you have been preparing for the success that lies ahead. The question is: Are you ready to take the leap? Chances are if you are reading this book right now, like Paul and Steve sitting around the barbecue grill, you daydream of more. You have goals yet to be realized, potential yet to be tapped, and dreams yet to be achieved.

Prep for Success: The Entrepreneur's Guide to Achieving your Dreams is designed to deliver the comprehensive business strategies you need, and is filled with engaging anecdotes and exciting opportunities for readers seeking to enter the orbit of Paul and Steve's remarkable experience and success. Here they share the six strategies required to take preparation to the next level:

- recognizing opportunity
- becoming a disruptor
- attracting talent
- establishing culture
- befriending Murphy
- embracing change

This book devotes chapters to each of these strategies. These comprehensive strategies put success in the crosshairs for professionals and entrepreneurs alike—those already in the hospitality industry, sales professionals, military personnel and spouses, daydreamers, virtually anyone looking to take control of their future once and for all—illustrating the power of prowess, preparation, and process to help you capitalize on unique opportunities to reach your ultimate potential ... and achieve your dreams!

Paul and Steve's serendipitous meeting and their subsequent remarkable successes were totally unplanned. This book, this moment may very well be *your* unplanned event, the chance you've been preparing for your whole life but never expected.

The time has come to *Prep for Success!*

Chapter One

ARE YOU READY?

• • • • • • • • • • • • • • • • • • • •

You will either step forward into growth,
or you will step back into safety.

—ABRAHAM MASLOW

Government contracts are kind of weird. When a government agency announces a request for proposal (RFP), bidders put together a proposal that describes their technical skills, training, past performance, pricing models, and lots of other details. It's an extremely complicated document that can easily take months to prepare. But the contract could lead to hundreds of thousands of dollars in business—or hundreds of *millions* of dollars. When you are ready, you hit "send" and then wait, and wait, and wait … You might not hear a peep for sometimes a month or two, then in a quick phone call you find out whether you won the contract.

Already running a very small, boutique event planning company at the time, Paul and Steve were vacationing together with their families in Breckenridge, Colorado, when that call came in 2007. They had rented a house, one of those massive ski homes that sleeps fourteen people. One afternoon the guys were out on the deck having a cold drink. Steve's phone rang. He looked down and saw a 202 area code: Washington, DC. He answered it.

"Yes, ma'am. Yes, ma'am. Yes, ma'am. Okay. Okay. Thank you."

Steve hung up and looked at Paul. "We won! We won!"

Paul and Steve's first big government contract was with the Defense Language Institute (DLI) out of Monterey, California, an $80,000 job. Steve was so excited that he picked up Paul and ran around the house with him, bouncing him up and down like he was a toddler.

At the time, they were novices, not really government contractors … not just yet. They were awarded the $80,000 contract, but they would not be paid until *after* the work was done. They had to finance everything up front: staff, uniforms, cell phones, computers, travel, even client expenses such as hotel, meals, audiovisual equipment, and printing. Steve used his AMEX card to pay for *everything*. Paul and Steve were definitely "mom and popping" it. But the government didn't know they were a mom-and-pop organization. They thought Paul and Steve were bona fide government contractors putting in a bid. Paul and Steve recognized the importance of that first big win, as their performance would build a solid foundation to grow their company. Failure was not an option!

FROM DAYDREAM TO REALITY

The $80,000 scramble all unfolded as the guys were ready to quasi-retire. Steve had left law enforcement to go into corporate America, and had become a vice president of operations for one of the largest youth training companies in Central Florida. Paul was still a cop and still in the National Guard as well. But he realized, after being in law enforcement for about four or five years, that while he loved the work and was good at it, he was never going to make a lot of money.

Paul's entrepreneurial brain was always trying to figure things out: *How do I advance to the rank of chief? How many steps and how much time would it take—sergeant, lieutenant, captain?* He knew he could climb that ladder over time, with education and experience. But when he looked at his military career, which he had already invested a big chunk of his life in, Paul realized his career had more potential if he went back on active duty.

The winds had changed a little, and the army at that time was looking to bring on more officers. Paul suddenly had the opportunity to transition back to active duty to finish out his career and earn a pension, so that's just what he did. They put him right into a place where he would be needed and had the most to offer: sales. The Army National Guard assigned Paul to the headquarters in Northern Virginia to be the chief of accessions (recruiting) for the country. He fit right in. It was something Paul had been doing most of his career, and very successfully. He'd been a field recruiter, but now it was time to take the leadership role and work on programs, budgets, policies—things that affected the nation, not just him as a recruiter.

His field recruiting mission goal was to sign up four people every month, which he nailed routinely. On his best month, Paul hit a dozen enlistments. Yet when he arrived at the National Guard

Bureau, his mission turned into seventy thousand enlistments per year. Of course, he didn't have to talk to them all individually; he just had to manage the process, systems, and resources available to get to that number.

The National Guard had about 4,500 recruiters, plus state managers, state officers, and state noncommissioned officers involved in the process that helped get recruits across the finish line. Paul oversaw all of that, as well as coordinating training events to bring them all together, from large and small conferences to workshops and awards banquets. Paul started getting very heavily involved with his staff in planning events, and it wasn't really what he was supposed to be doing. After all, Paul wasn't an event planner. He was supposed to be leading recruiting for the Army National Guard.

At this point, Steve happened to be engaged in multistate operations just like Paul. The two were traveling extensively, and gaining tons of event experience. Paul was traveling to different states, training people, hiring people, and growing the force. What he was doing on the governmental side, Steve was doing on the commercial side. Paul just kept noticing the redundancy of what they were doing, the commonality of the hotel negotiations, the hotel requirements, the logistical planning, the audiovisual needs, the transportation, the speakers, the catering, the registration, the staffing. Paul was spending a lot of money on those events. He thought to himself one day: *Wow, if I was a civilian and I owned an event planning company, I could make a fortune working for my department.* But of course he couldn't do anything about his idea because it would have been a conflict of interest.

But the more he kept thinking about all those events, the more the idea drove him crazy. Every department and division of the government, from aviation safety to maintenance and medical, has conferences. *Thousands* of conferences. And when Paul started looking at the firms that were managing them, he saw the talent pool was pretty shallow. The companies doing it were either extremely small with a lot of capabilities, or very large companies that really weren't event planners at all; they were just big government contractors that could be whatever you wanted them to be for the right price.

Paul kept thinking there should be some middle-sized company that not only had the talent, but also the capacity and bandwidth to simultaneously deliver multiple events in multiple cities. Not to mention have the cash-flow resources on hand to deliver services and wait for the government to reimburse them a couple months later, because there's usually a delay in government payment.

Steve happened to be in Hawaii when Paul called one day. This was probably the tenth time Paul had called Steve with some crazy idea, but Steve was always willing to listen. Paul was extremely excited. "All right, I think I got our next thing." Then he started pitching Steve the event planning concept, with training workshops and seminars, which was exactly what both happened to be heavily involved in at the time.

Steve saw the merit in the idea right away. Whether it was the National Association of the Chiefs of Police, or recruiters for the military, he knew very well they all had meetings and conferences. Medical professionals have meetings and conferences. No matter what the profession, they could replicate the process and the system to manage all kinds of workshops and training sessions. If they designed it properly, they could simply have a plug-and-play service that fit most clients' needs.

The friends kept tossing the idea around and agreed to meet in Florida. Paul put together a five- page PowerPoint deck and they sat around the coffee table mulling it all over. Then, in an effort to identify their "why" for the business, Paul asked, "What's our exit strategy?" Steve couldn't help but laugh. "Exit strategy? We haven't even started yet."

After hours of careful thought and discussion, they decided to do it. Paul and Steve each threw in $1,500, opened a bank account, and bought the website www.nationalconference.com, which is now the parent company of Federal Conference and a sister company to EventPrep.

THE EARLY HUSTLE

With $3,000 and sweat equity, they knew it all would start with a single event. Initially they shared the role of CEO—chief *everything* officer. They weren't necessarily technically proficient, but they built the online registration site. They did all the administrative work, accounting, sales, marketing, graphic design, printing, and execution of every detail.

Paul and Steve built an organizational chart that reflected what they thought "right" looked like. Not right for those days, but right for where they were headed. That chart had a bunch of empty squares on it, because it was just them, after all. They had to say, "All right, which jobs are you going to put your name on until we can start hiring?" Steve was doing two or three jobs. Paul was doing two or three jobs. They were throwing the football back and forth to each other just to score a touchdown.

When it came to showtime, their first event, Steve and Paul took a vacation from their full-time jobs. They literality went on site to deliver their services and clean up the mess, and then came back to home base. They'd high-five each other and laugh about the lessons learned, brag about the successes. But they weren't making any money. They basically just generated enough revenue to cover the trip out there and pay for their cell phones. At that point they didn't really have a structure. They were working out of their home offices in their pajamas. Yet all the while they were experimenting with what worked and what didn't; they were learning and refining their process, fine-tuning it to become the well-oiled machine it is today.

Federal Conference began with one event. Before long came the second one. Then number three. They must have been through a dozen or so events together, hustling like mad and getting a battle rhythm down ... when suddenly they had two events on the same weekend. Now they had to be in two different places at one time, and that was when Paul and Steve looked at each other and realized the training wheels were off. They couldn't depend on each other anymore. So Steve went off to handle one event while Paul went off to handle another. Things started to get interesting at that point because it became very competitive about whose event was better. A little friendly rivalry between Fred and Barney.

They did that for a while, learning and growing ... and then they faced a trifecta weekend: three events at the same time. That's when they knew they needed to expand and start making different types of decisions. They had to bring in new talent and trust them with their baby.

THE STAGES OF GROWTH

There's a concept in business of measured growth, just like stages of human development: infancy, adolescence, and maturity. Every business starts in infancy. And, just as with raising children, it's logistically difficult to execute. It takes constant nurturing, constant monitoring, hands-on attention at all times. But it's the passion that drives you through most of your pain and suffering.

If you've done your job properly, your business will graduate into adolescence. And just like with a teenager, the adolescent years are usually the hardest because they are emotionally difficult. The problems are more challenging, but there's some sense of stability and autonomy. But, just as with a teenager, if you walked away from it for a while, it might seem okay at first, but would self-implode sooner or later.

At this stage, leaders usually start delegating more to others. They relinquish more of the control to make decisions and take action. With delegating and trusting people comes a degree of risk, however, and this is where many leaders make a fatal mistake. Not because of trusting others, but because of *not* allowing the growing pains of the adolescence stage. Instead of dealing with the errors that inevitably will occur, many business owners will pull back and take on more responsibility—responsibility they didn't have the bandwidth to deal with in the first place, which was why they started delegating. This causes regression back to infancy, and can eventually lead to overall failure.

A mature company is defined as no longer needing the owner(s) to be physically present daily for it to be successful. Competent leadership is in place and there are proven systems and processes to follow. While EventPrep is still an emerging brand, Federal Conference is a good example of a mature company.

GETTING RESOURCEFUL ON A SHOESTRING

In those very early days of moving from infancy to adolescence, Paul and Steve didn't have a robust staff, just two guys with vision, passion, and determination. But for events like the ones they started delivering, they needed additional help: customer service-savvy conference attendants who could greet the attendees, hand out name badges, assist with registration, and help with the millions of little details that go into event planning. Imagine being in a strange city and trying to put on a conference. Where do you find temporary, quality help in a hurry?

If they had gone through Craigslist, hiring people sight unseen, the guys could be taking a huge risk. They were dealing with a very specific kind of audience: military folks, high-ranking officers, professionals. It wasn't Paul and Steve's event after all; it was *the client's* event. And they couldn't risk having someone show up who was unpresentable or unprofessional. They needed people who would know how to put their best foot forward, that smiling, welcoming, we-can-help-you-customer service model. For each event, they needed a small army of quality folks who reflected their culture, and more importantly, their clients' culture.

Paul and Steve recognized that they had a staffing dilemma and needed to come up with an affordable solution quickly. One day, while eating lunch at a local establishment, they noticed a correlation between their server's skills and their current staffing needs. They also realized they didn't need to reinvent a customer service model because it already existed in most major cities where their events were being delivered.

Most chain restaurants have really good training programs for their staff, and they nurture great customer service skills. So Paul and Steve would intentionally fly in a couple days early and head right for a local chain restaurant. They'd ask for the manager, present their business cards, and tell him that they were in town to deliver a big event and were interested in hiring some local talent. They needed professional, presentable, capable people who could come in and wear their branded shirts, khakis, and comfortable shoes; hand out name badges; monitor rooms; help attendees find the restrooms; direct the flow of traffic; stuff tote bags—whatever was needed. They needed temporary brand ambassadors.

Paul and Steve would pick two or three staff members and pay them $200 a day to work the event. Suddenly they had an army of really sharp, presentable, customer service-oriented, friendly people. All the guys had to do was figure out what it was they wanted them to do and provide a little training.

They would meet with the new recruits for four hours before the event started, issue uniforms, and talk about standards, the brand, and what was acceptable. There was no sitting around. If someone walked up, those temporary brand ambassadors knew to stand up and greet them. Paul and Steve tapped into a ready-made talent pool so they didn't have to reinvent it. And to this day, many of those folks still work with them in cities across the country.

That model really helped set the stage for success for the determined duo. Their clients just loved the staff. Wearing Paul and Steve's shirts and logos, they seemed to be part of the family, and they became one of the key assets their event planning company could bring to the table.

JUST A FEW MORE ZEROES

And then the $80,000 contract happened. After they were awarded it, Steve and Paul knew they needed to make some big decisions. It was a huge responsibility that would require a significant investment in time and resources to manage, especially if they wanted to make a name for themselves. So they both started burning some serious midnight oil, working two jobs and raising their families to boot, and really focused on building the business.

Over time, the guys grew tired of the one-offs and sporadic little fish. They wanted to go fishing every day... and go after even bigger fish.

By the spring of 2010, through all the effort and momentum they had built, they had made their first $1 million after being awarded a multimillion-dollar contract with the navy. What led to this avalanche of success? It's important to note that the guys didn't necessarily invent event planning; they just built a better mousetrap. They catered to their customers' needs and built something they thought was of value to their customers. And then they kept on replicating and building. Every time Paul and Steve learned a lesson, they implemented it across the board, across all of their operations.

Paul's gifts were sales, marketing, and administration. Steve's were operations and delivery.

Suddenly the time came when they had to hire their first employee. Up until then, they had several independent contractors, known as 1099 employees. But when the first W-2 employee finally arrived, those three years that followed brought explosive growth.

By 2011 they were handling forty to fifty events a year all over the US. They were traveling. They were negotiating hotels in every major city. They were building relationships and a reputation. They were making top-line revenue just north of $2 million a year.

And then Paul and Steve saw a huge contracting opportunity come from the army. It would be a Hail Mary attempt. The work had previously gone to a larger contractor, but it was coming up for rebid. Paul looked at the requirements and found it was very similar to a navy contract they had. The only thing different was the volume. Where the guys were doing forty or fifty events a year, that particular contract called for more than *three thousand* events a year.

They put together a written proposal that was more like a college thesis. It took them weeks to write. Paul was working from home at the time, trying to write this thing that he didn't even know the value of yet because they had to do a very complex cost estimate. His kids were young at the time: seven, eight, and ten. Every few minutes they were running into Paul's home office, asking, "Dad, do you want to go outside and play baseball? Dad, can you come down and make me a sandwich? Dad, where's Mom? Dad, Dad, Dad."

Finally, Paul said, "Kids, you've got to leave me alone. I'm working on something very important here. I know it looks like I'm at home right now, but I'm not. I'm working on a very big contract, and if I win this, it's going to make millions of dollars. And if we make millions of dollars ... I will give each of you a thousand dollars. So just please leave me alone and let me write this proposal."

Huge parenting mistake. Granted, Paul could have gotten away with five dollars, but he was desperate. He wasn't really even sure they were going to win the thing, but the guys were determined to give it the old college try. They went through a routine they still practice—saying a little prayer before hitting "send." You might think it would be to ask God to win the bid, but instead they always ask that God's will be done, as they understand that any outcome impacts so many lives. After all, if they win, an incumbent loses.

Finally they submitted the proposal. Then they waited. And waited. A couple of weeks went by. Steve and Paul were sitting at his kitchen table when Paul's phone rang. As with the call a couple years earlier, he looked at this one and his heart quickened at the sight of the 202 area code: Washington, DC.

Paul glanced at Steve. "This is it. This is the call. Are you ready?"

"No. Come on. Stop playing with me," Steve said.

"I'm not. This is the contracting office." Paul answered the phone. "Hello." The lady on the other end said, "Mr. Trapp, I have a question for you in reference to your proposal."

Paul tried as hard as he could to remain calm. "All right, ma'am. How can I help you?"

"Well, it says here in your proposal that you're a small business. Because you're a small business, you'll need to do a quick-pay process that the government has. I understand you want to be able to submit an invoice every week to get paid to keep your cash flow going. Unfortunately, I'm not able to do that. The best I could possibly do would be two weeks. Would that be okay with you?"

Paul swallowed hard and said, "Ma'am, are you telling me that if I agree to the two-week payment program, we've got the contract?"

"Yes. That's what I'm telling you."

Paul probably should have consulted Steve, but he didn't think his friend would mind. "I agree to the two-week payment cycle."

"Well, great," she said. "I will be sending you a contract shortly. I just need to get it finalized and send it over for signature."

The guys had just won an $81 million contract. That day Steve couldn't pick Paul up because he was near cardiac arrest. All they needed to do at that point was execute.

After all, killing the elephant is the easy part ... getting it out of the jungle is where it gets tricky.

FRANCHISEE SPOTLIGHT: DANIELLE MARLAR, CGMP

About Danielle:

Born and raised in Northern Virginia, I am thirty years old and live in Haymarket, Virginia, with my husband and two dogs. I am the oldest of four with two brothers and one sister. I spent my later years growing up in Loudoun County, Virginia, where I met my husband. We recently moved back to Prince William County in 2017, where we bought our first home. Luckily both our families are still relatively close by. I grew up in a very competitive home that focused on academics and sports. My siblings and I all played high school sports and enjoy watching NFL games together on Sundays. I attended George Mason University, where I studied interpersonal communications and tourism and events management. After college, I got a job as an events coordinator at a private golf course in Haymarket, coordinating weddings, golf outings, and other social events. I worked there for roughly four years and then transitioned over to Federal Conference with Paul and Steve as an event planner for the army. After a year and a half of event planning, I was promoted to an event manager and began to manage a team of event planners under the army contract.

Where did you hear about EventPrep?

Having worked for Paul and Steve for three years under Federal Conference, they kept me in the loop as they started the EventPrep journey. As soon as I heard it was coming to fruition, I knew it was something I needed to do!

What motivated you to become a franchisee?

I was recently married, had purchased my first home, and felt like it was the right time to take a chance on my career. Event planning has always been a passion of mine and it seemed like this opportunity had fallen into my lap at such a perfect time in my life. As soon as Paul and Steve were approved to sell in Virginia, I gave my notice and was ready to be a business owner.

I had my initial interview for Federal Conference with Steve. He was so welcoming, with lots of energy and confidence that I would be success-ful in his company. Steve was the heart of Federal Conference. He made me laugh on a daily basis and I could always go to him for support. I wasn't as close with Paul my first year at the company, but slowly got to know him more as I grew with the company. Paul became my mentor. I sat in his office many days learning from him —about sales, what motivates people, how to manage people, and how to keep customers happy. I learned so much from Paul and in fact still call him for advice and guidance. Paul and Steve attended my wedding, and we've traveled together for work, but they are great lifelong friends as well, and are a very big part of where I am today in my career.

What were factors in your decision to become a franchisee?

The driving factor was knowing that I had the support of my Federal Conference team, friends, and family. I have always been motivated by money and thought someday I would probably end up in sales. My father and husband are both in sales, so I suppose it's always been a part of my everyday life. I was taught that if you can do an eight-hour day of work in four, then why not do it for yourself and make twice the amount. But my true passion has always been to help people, and by that I mean in a more social/creative way, such as planning someone's wedding, or an annual conference for a company, or a training event for military soldiers. EventPrep allows me to do that and also provides a financial incentive.

How is your life today as a franchisee?

Life is good! The first year was an adventure. I learned a lot, and reflected a lot. I know it takes time to grow a business, but I do think my first year was a success and I had a lot of support from Paul and Steve along the way. I have a better work-life balance, and am able to grow my business in the direction I want it to go. Adjusting to working from home all day every day has been tough, but I get quite a lot done and enjoy spending time doing things I didn't think I would or could do as an employee. I feel healthy and happy, and know that I am taking time for myself, my family, and friends, and at the same time running and growing my own business at thirty years old.

Chapter Two

PREP FOR SUCCESS

● ● ● ● ● ● ● ● ● ● ● ● ● ● ● ● ● ● ● ●

Luck is what happens when preparation meets opportunity.

—SENECA, ROMAN PHILOSOPHER

How do you stay alive on the street as a cop? How do you feed, shelter, and protect people affected by disaster and destruction as a member of the National Guard? How do you function under high-stress conditions when the worst-case scenario becomes reality? The answer to those questions is the same as the answer to the old adage: How do you get to Carnegie Hall? Practice, practice, practice. You may be born with some natural ability, a particular talent, or a survival instinct, but the only way you learn and grow and perfect that ability is through repetition.

As law enforcement officers, Paul and Steve constantly trained, trained, and trained some more. They went to the police academy.

They went to the shooting range. They were always in some type of class to level up and hone their skills because when the time came, they needed to be ready for anything and everything.

When Steve was the leader of the SWAT team, he had to be prepared for the worst when he executed a search warrant. Whenever he entered a zone or a building, he couldn't just walk up and open the door. The training started weeks or months earlier in preparation for a specific planned event … and the *unplanned* event, that unfortunate moment when things suddenly go sideways. With officer safety a top priority, nothing could be assumed. Not one shred of information that came in was beyond scrutiny. The plan was created and practiced long before the actual execution of the warrant.

The same holds true for the military. Preparedness is the key in any and all situations. When Steve was assigned to a dignitary protection team in Iraq, he had to make sure no harm came to the generals or the secretary of defense when they visited. When Paul and Steve were deployed to Germany and a general came for a visit, they were ready because they had prepared weeks in advance for the event. They found out where the general wanted to go, who he wanted to talk to, and what his agenda was. Then they did an advance recon before the general ever set foot in theater. They visited every single place the general wanted to go. They looked every person in the eye whom he wanted to meet with. They researched emergency egresses, and identified the hospitals in case things went sideways. The level of detail in preparation for such an event is beyond imagination. Speaking to the surgical nurse? Yes. Speaking to the doctors on staff? Yep. Determining the level of hospital care: level one, level two, level three? If not there, then where?

PREPAREDNESS IS THE KEY IN ANY AND ALL SITUATIONS.

What are the routes? Alternate routes? How long does it take to get there? All the above, and more.

Look at the sports world. Can you imagine if the Patriots showed up on the field Super Bowl Sunday and said, "We haven't practiced in a year. Let's try to put something together here and win the game." How many drills do they go through at that level? How many videos do they watch? How many practices do they have? Do they have a playbook?

EVERY SINGLE EVENT IN LIFE IS A SUPER BOWL IF YOU REALLY WANT TO BE SUCCESSFUL.

Every single event in life is a Super Bowl if you really want to be successful. The key to mastering the art of preparation is practice and having a playbook.

PLAYBOOKS

In the military, all unit members know when they get the encrypted phone call with a message like, "The cows are out in the pasture," that means they're all heading to the armory within twelve or twenty-four hours, bags packed, ready to go. You need to have all your affairs in order. You better have a will made. You better have a child-care plan. You better have arranged for your bills to be paid while you're gone. These are things the military trains every soldier to do before the word "war" or "deployment" even comes up. A legal team provides advice. The military even brings in dentists to examine your teeth because it doesn't want to send you to war with a toothache.

To keep all of these millions of details organized so all can be executed seamlessly and flawlessly, the military creates a series of playbooks called mobilization books. These three-ring binders lay out the entire mobilization plan prior to the mobilization. They determine which officer/NCO is going to be responsible for supplies during mobilization, along with a checklist of tasks for that supply officer. So the second we get called into action, the right person is showing up, pulling his checklist out, drawing a basic load of ammunition for everyone there, basic food rations, provisions, and all other equipment needed. The maintenance officer springs into action making sure all the vehicles are up and running, doing primary maintenance checks on them. The cooks are preparing rations and planning to make meals on the fly, without a kitchen.

When tragedy strikes, you can't just make it up as you go along. You go right for the mobilization book and start running through the checklists. Every major catastrophe or event has a book to go with it, from a terrorist attack to a hurricane to a nuclear plant meltdown, with details down to the smallest degree. Why wouldn't a business have a similar plan?

All of this preparation experience while serving our country prepared Paul and Steve to succeed as businessmen ... and to deliver on a sudden $81 million contract.

PREPPING FOR "WHAT IF"

When Paul hit "submit" on that proposal, it was like little David launching that small stone from his slingshot at the lumbering giant, Goliath. Immediately the buddies sprang into action for the "what if" scenario and started to build their playbook, just in case their aim was true and happened to slay the beast.

Because the guys didn't have enough staff on hand to deliver on a contract of that magnitude, they had to estimate a few things. For personnel, they identified the number of employees and skill sets required based on the minimum criteria Paul had built into the proposal. Then they created job descriptions and took ads out on LinkedIn, Indeed, and Craigslist. Without even an office, Paul and Steve had to meet candidates in a Panera Bread location for the job interview. When they found someone who fit the bill for a particular position, they offered employment contingent on being granted the contract. They did this approximately fifty times, for approximately fifty staff members, from senior leadership with six-figure salaries all the way down.

They took the same tactic when it came to equipment. The little HP printer/copier/scanner combo that fit on Paul's desktop wasn't going to suffice for planning and executing three thousand events a year and thousands of copies every day. Neither would his small wastebasket-style shredder. They needed real, corporate office equipment. So they shopped for what they expected to need, and they negotiated a lease on a copier and other necessities like thirty-five smartphones ... all contingent on the "what if" scenario.

Steve and Paul also knew they couldn't operate a high-functioning business out of Steve's kitchen with thirty to forty new employees, so they started looking for office space. They met with Realtors and building owners, toured endless sites and office spaces, and ultimately signed an agreement to take possession ... *if* they were awarded the contract.

Finally they were prepared to transition from mom-and-pop to corporate America in a minute's notice. And then that minute arrived.

After Paul picked Steve up off the floor and dusted him off, the guys pulled out the playbooks. They delegated tasks and started making calls to the building owner, the office supply company, the employees waiting in the wings. They finalized contracts, set up meetings, and scheduled deliveries. The call from the government happened on a Friday; by the following Monday, people were reporting for duty at Steve's home. The office space wasn't quite ready, so the new IT director was opening boxes of computers in the basement. There weren't any desks yet, so he stacked computer boxes on top of each other so he could log in all the serial numbers for all the other computers and start the network. Twenty to thirty staff members needed a place to do their work, so every room in the house became an office space, including the picnic table in the backyard.

By Wednesday of that week, Paul and Steve had their first meeting with their new client, George. The guys were so proud of their plan and went about sharing it with him when suddenly he slid everything over to the side and said, "That's all good and dandy. Nice plan. Let's hold those for another discussion. Here's a list of eighty-five events that are starting this Friday."

That's when everything got real for Paul and Steve. Eighty-five events. In two days. All over the US. Planning, executing, locating hotels, negotiating contracts, catering, audiovisual, all of it. Everything. But Paul and Steve were prepared. They had the people, they had the equipment, they had the plan. Getting it all done, however, came down to a valuable, yet simple lesson in volleyball.

BUMP, SET, SPIKE

Steve and Paul, needless to say, were a little stressed. They were trying to be cool and calm, but failure at the starting line was not an option. So they took a walk to clear their heads and focus on how to execute. They headed down to the beach, where they sat, talked, and watched a bunch of kids playing volleyball.

Their initial proposal factored in a transition period for the massive volume of events, perhaps thirty to sixty days to get acclimated to the process. Certainly not two days. They had to go back to their makeshift office, round up their new team, and break the news. They couldn't stick to the original plan of twenty steps or the team would get confused, not keep the steps in the right order, and likely drown. They needed to give them a new plan of action, something simple and easily digestible.

They were contemplating all of this while watching this volleyball game, and Paul and Steve kept hearing the kids yell out: "Bump, set, spike! Bump, set, spike!" And the players were following orders exactly. That rhythm was the essence of preparation. The ball comes over the net. The guy in the back row dives to the dirt and gets his hand underneath the ball right before it touches the ground and bumps it up. He doesn't try to get it over the net. He just tries to get it off the ground. That's his only task. And then the player in the second row realizes there's a ball in play about eye level, and he sets it forward to the guy in the front row, who spikes it over the net. They planned that move. They talked about it before they did it. Bump, set, spike!

That's when Paul and Steve realized one of the great lessons in life was to keep it simple. A, B, C, 1, 2, 3. In volleyball, it's bump, set, spike. So the guys ended up rolling the twenty steps of the original plan into bump, set, spike.

THAT'S WHEN PAUL AND STEVE REALIZED ONE OF THE GREAT LESSONS IN LIFE WAS TO KEEP IT SIMPLE. A, B, C, 1, 2, 3. IN VOLLEYBALL, IT'S BUMP, SET, SPIKE.

Back at the house, Paul took a flip chart and a felt marker and Steve rallied everyone into one room, where they crowded onto chairs, couches, and the floor. Then the two started assigning people to groups. The Bumps were given a list of tasks and that would be their sole focus: reach out to the customer, gather basic information, and confirm all the information for hotels, location, transportation, curriculum, child care, food and beverage, and audiovisual needs.

When finished, the Bumps would hand the checklist to the Sets. The Setters were divided into several smaller groups, one solely responsible for transportation, one for food and beverage, one for curriculum.

The Spikes were the managers, who oversaw quality control. They reviewed and signed the contracts and finalized all the details.

Paul and Steve literally provided little stick-on name badges that read: Hi, I'm Bump. Hi, I'm Set. Hi, I'm Spike. That was all the guys wanted them to know. And it worked. They survived. And they went on to execute a battle rhythm of eighty events each week, week after week.

PREPARATION AIN'T PRETTY

Preparation isn't the sexy part of the job. Think back to our Super Bowl analogy and all the glory, the pomp and circumstance, the ring, the championship. How many hours, days, weeks, months did the winning team spend preparing for that? There's no glory in the 4:00 a.m. wakeup calls, all the practices, all the losses, all the sacrifices, and all the grime and dirt and pain and injuries. To win a big trial, experienced litigation lawyers don't solely focus on their fifteen-minute closing remarks. They spend months leading up to that first day of court, when they research the case law, study, and put their plan together to win their case.

Everything is about that preparation. The $81 million contract Paul and Steve won was terrific. But it came with an enormous amount of hard work both before and after winning the contract. It's not the Super Bowl ring that you should be focused on. It's all of the work leading up to it. Because if you don't do all of that work leading up to it, you'll never get to the Super Bowl.

And that $81 million contract was like winning the Super Bowl for Paul and Steve. Like New England Patriots quarterback Tom Brady and his multiple Super Bowl rings, over the years they've been awarded that same contract four times as of this writing—with each contract worth anywhere from $60 million to $144 million.

But that's what happens when preparation intersects with opportunity, as well as when you leverage the six strategies required to take preparation to the next level: seizing opportunity, becoming a disruptor, attracting talent, establishing culture, befriending Murphy, and embracing change.

Let's take a deeper dive into each one, and see how Paul and Steve used these strategies to achieve their dreams.

FRANCHISEE SPOTLIGHT: ALISON DAVIS

About Alison:

I am fifty-three years old, married, with two sons, ten and twelve, and I live in Woodbine, Maryland. I have been in the hospitality industry for more than twenty-five years. I became a meeting planner nine years ago with another company because I wanted the flexibility of working from home while caring for my boys, who were babies at the time.

Where did you hear about EventPrep?

After my first year with HelmsBriscoe (HB), I had the pleasure of being part of a team that worked on the Federal Conference account and army contract events. That is how I met Paul, Steve, and Denise. I absolutely loved working with them and for them. After two years of working on army contract events, the account went away due to government sequestration. I continued to stay in touch with Paul, Steve, and Denise. Still with HB, the army account returned after a two-year hiatus and I was working with Paul and Steve once again. I was thrilled. I loved working on these events, not only because I enjoyed working with Federal

Conference, but because I find assisting military families in some way very rewarding.

After a year, the Army Strong Bonds (ASB) disappeared again. At that point, Federal Conference made a business decision to bring site selection in house. Although I certainly understood, I was so upset. I reached out to Paul and asked if he would hire me, as I wanted to work for them. Our business relationship had grown over the years and I really wanted to be a part of their team. But the timing was not right as they were restricted by a noncompete agreement with HB.

What motivated you to become a franchisee?

Paul and I continued to talk. We met various times as EventPrep was being developed, and he started to share their vision. I wanted in. It was an incredible opportunity and I would get to work with them again. That's when I became an EventPrep franchisee.

What were factors in your decision to become a franchisee?

I have the utmost respect for Paul, Steve, and Denise. I *get* them ... and their vision. I love that not only was I making more in commission, but they had a startup program for the first year. When I left HB, I also had a noncompete clause and was unable to solicit my existing clients, so I had to start from scratch. But that was okay, because I knew it was the right thing to do.

How is your life today as a franchisee?

It was absolutely the best day of my life when I became a franchisee. It has been life changing. Not one regret.

What is the best part of being a franchisee?

Everything!

Chapter Three

RECOGNIZING OPPORTUNITY

• •

A pessimist sees the difficulty in the opportunity; an optimist sees opportunity in every difficulty.

—SIR WINSTON CHURCHILL

Imagine for a moment that Paul and Steve are at forty thousand feet, en route to New York to plan an event for one of their clients. Steve is near the window, Paul has an aisle seat, and a random passenger named Bill has the dreaded middle seat. Paul turns to Bill to make a little conversation. "So are you headed to New York for business or pleasure?"

"New York is home for me. What about you guys?" replies Bill.

Steve says, "Were doing a big, weeklong event in Manhattan."

Bill lights up. "Oh, well I'm actually just coming back from our big event. We were down in Orlando. I own a company that puts on a major event every year."

Paul and Steve exchange glances. "Really?" says Paul. "That's funny because we happen to be event planners. So who exactly plans your events?"

Bill smiles. "Suzy, my administrative assistant."

Steve chimes in. "Is she an event planner?"

"Well, not by trade, but by default. It's one of her additional duties," says Bill.

Paul then asks, "How does Suzy find hotels?"

Bill shrugs. "I tell her I want to be in Central Florida, she goes to Google and starts to search for hotels in Central Florida. She starts dialing, talking to the salespeople, writes it all down on a notepad, then comes in, briefs me, and we pick one."

That's when Paul says, "Okay, well that's clearly one way to do it. But maybe it's not the best way to monetize it, or the best way to save money, or the best way to make sure your event is a success. By the way, Bill, how do you define success for your event?"

So the guys are basically asking Bill questions. It's just a conversation. They've not sold him anything. He owns a company that does events. But Paul and Steve know he could be getting a better deal. They know he could have the entire process running more efficiently with even better experience for his attendees, smoother registration, and higher-end amenities for himself and his leadership team. He's a guy who has a need he didn't realize he had. Paul and Steve are slowly and expertly leading him to that realization, and with it comes the knowledge that their services won't cost him a penny.

Imagine you meet someone who can help you solve a need because he or she has the tools, technology, information, experience, and education to get it done quicker, better, stronger, and faster … with fewer bruises, bumps, scrapes, and cuts along the way. Plus that person will protect you and not charge you a cent.

Where have we seen this model before?

THE REAL ESTATE AGENT MODEL

Recognizing opportunity is one thing. Having the ability and taking the initiative to *seize* it is something altogether different. And the key to seizing an opportunity is identifying a need greater than your own: that of your customer. As a business owner, you have many needs: personnel needs, supply needs, payroll needs, and scaling needs, just to name a few. But by and large all of those needs come down to one very simple need: money. People are in business to make money, which ultimately is the vehicle to getting all other needs met. The customer, however, can have a plethora of needs, and not one of them involves paying you money. So how do you unlock an opportunity to make money by satisfying someone's need if that person isn't willing to pay you? Convince the customer of a need the person didn't realize he or she had, then get a third party to pay for it.

THE KEY TO SEIZING AN OPPORTUNITY IS IDENTIFYING A NEED GREATER THAN YOUR OWN.

Think about what real estate agents do for home buyers. They meet with the future homeowners, perhaps at their kitchen table, and ask, "What's important to you and your spouse in your future home?" Then the Realtor shuts up and listens. Maybe some items on the wish list include having enough yard space for the kids to play.

Or because one of the clients travels a lot, they want to be close to the airport. Or maybe they need something with a fenced-in backyard for the pets. Or a ranch-style home because stairs would be too much for the client with a knee injury. Or maybe it's all of the above.

The Realtor takes notes, asks more questions, takes more notes, and finally creates a vision of the perfect house for the clients. Then the agent will likely go back to the office and plug the criteria into the Multiple Listing Service (MLS), a real estate technology platform that all Realtors have access to. Before long, the Realtor has a detailed list of homes that match, complete with images, prices, square footages, school districts, and all the amenities.

Another meeting with the clients may whittle the list down even further based on taste and preference. Then the Realtor will walk them through the homes that made the short list, narrowing down the final options even more. During these walk-throughs, the agent is pointing out the advantages and disadvantages of each home from an expert's perspective. Agents know what's happening in their lane, things like whether construction in the neighborhood will be going on for the next three years, or if there is an unresolved drainage issue, or if car theft rates have been unusually high in the area. The agent is looking out for the clients and wants to help them make a good decision.

Once clients choose a house, the agent starts the next phase of the job representing them by pulling comps, sorting through the details, and negotiating a fair asking price based not only on the market, but on invaluable experience. The agent walks the clients through every step of the process, explaining every detail, and acting in their best interest all the way through the closing. The agent might even send the new homeowners a "thank you for trusting me with your business" card, complete with a restaurant gift card to celebrate their new house.

And how does that agent get paid for all that hard work? A commission split with the seller's agent. The buyers never had to pay a penny.

That's exactly the model Paul and Steve have perfected to serve their clients through Federal Conference and EventPrep.

A MODEL EVENT

While brokering a home sale involves permanent lodging, brokering an event involves temporary lodging. Clients are only going to be there for a few days to a week, possibly ten days. An individual simply attending an event wouldn't necessarily need the power and leverage of an event planning company to get a flight and hotel room. But when we're talking about conventions, trade shows, corporate meetings and conferences, symposia, weddings, fraternal organization get-togethers, nonprofit galas, government agency events, and team sporting events, they all need to be coordinated and organized to be executed efficiently and successfully. So who's organizing them? Chances are no one. A high school soccer trip, for example, might follow an "every person for him- or herself" approach, with everyone going through Expedia and booking a room separately. Just imagine that: twenty athletes and their families staying in twenty different hotels at twenty different price points.

But what if someone could organize that event and bring them all together, negotiate the rate at one hotel to bring the bulk business there, and then set it up and put out the information so all the parents funnel through one place? Suddenly they get a discount from $119 per night to $99 per night, plus breakfast and private use of a conference room. What?! But why? Because the hotel wants that kind of bulk, and potentially repeat, business. And when a hotel wants your business, all sorts of benefits can be negotiated.

THE POWER OF RELATIONSHIPS

Let's revisit our analogy of New York business owner Bill on the plane. Just like with the Realtor, the more questions Paul and Steve ask Bill, the closer they begin to dial into his needs, whether he is aware of them or not. Before long they find out that he likes to have his annual company event at a different location each year, plus he throws a few regional conferences every so often. In the winter he likes his attendees to be able to go skiing in a place like Aspen. In the summer, he prefers Walt Disney World.

The guys learn how many attendees usually show up for each event, which tells them how many beds they'll need to negotiate. And like the Realtor creating a client wish list, Paul and Steve start itemizing Bill's conference needs: audiovisual equipment for four days, one large conference room and several smaller rooms for breakout sessions, food and beverage, and a celebratory dinner the final night.

What Bill doesn't realize is that because Paul and Steve spend tens of millions of dollars each year with the major hotel brands, they get preferred pricing that he or his administrative assistant could never get for their single event. Paul and Steve use the collective purchasing power of *all* their clients, not just Bill. Bill is going to do an event once or twice a year at a Hyatt or a Hilton or Marriott. Since their inception, Paul and Steve have spent hundreds of millions of dollars with the major hotel chains, so when Paul and Steve call to plan an event at a hotel, they receive an entirely different welcome than the occasional customer. The guys can unlock doors, negotiate terms, and get perks thrown in that Suzy could never get.

After the plane lands, Paul grabs Bill's business card and the guys begin doing their thing. Like the Realtor lining up a set of listings for the client to evaluate, Paul and Steve put together the best deals and negotiate all the bells and whistles possible for Bill to consider. Remember, Bill hasn't paid Paul and Steve a dime, but the guys have already leveraged their relationship power to present Bill with all he needs to make an informed decision. They've gotten one hotel to agree to provide a wine and cheese reception for all the attendees the night the event begins, while another hotel is throwing in rounds of golf for the VIPs and transportation to and from the airport.

Eventually Paul and Steve call Bill and tell him they're going to email the five bids from the hotels all fighting to host his events. Just like a Realtor, Paul and Steve walk Bill through each quote and offer their professional opinions of the offers, helping to guide Bill toward a decision that is best for him. Remember, Bill is going to have these events anyway, so what does he do when he sees that every one of them is not only going to be less expensive, but will include amazing perks he never thought of … not to mention make him look great to his attendees? All without having to pay Paul and Steve a penny?

It's a no-brainer. But wait … there's more!

THE ROYAL TREATMENT

Just like a Realtor, Paul and Steve meet people. They listen to what people say they need. They capture those needs, then they plug them into a technology platform and get a list of results for the client to consider. But what would happen if the sellers of the homes under consideration sweetened the pot by pampering the potential home buyers? That's exactly what happens in Paul and Steve's business.

Those hotels desperately want events involving three hundred or five hundred people staying for a week. They stand to make tremendous amounts of money just from one event. How badly do they want that business?

So badly that the hotel contact will call Paul and Steve and ask, "Hey guys, has Bill made a decision yet?" To which the guys will reply, "No, he's still on the fence. In fact, he's looking at two other hotels in the area." The hotel representative then says something like, "Well, why don't we have Bill fly out here and we'll show him our property. We'll wine and dine Bill and his staff. Tell him to bring Suzy his assistant with him. We'll have Chef Pierre come out of the kitchen and cook his famous recipes. We'll do a chef's tasting. We'll let him play a round of golf. We'll get him a massage. We'll put him up in the president's suite. And it's all free. We just want him to come see our property, because we think if he sees our property, and gets this VIP experience, he's gonna want to do his event here." And ironically the other two hotels are courting the client in a similar fashion.

So now all of a sudden, Paul and Steve are talking to Bill about not just looking at the best deal with the most perks, but about these hotels vying for his event so badly they are willing to send a car to pick him up at the airport and treat him and his staff to a VIP experience for a couple days.

Definitely something Suzy wouldn't have known to do.

A NOTE ABOUT SUZY

The analogy with Bill illustrates the process of seizing opportunity where seemingly none existed, and you may be concerned that Suzy, Bill's administrative assistant, might feel suddenly left out. In building their model, Paul and Steve understood the true psychology behind this dynamic. With them swooping in and saving the day, they risk Suzy feeling like part of her job has been taken away. In a way, Paul and Steve almost become a threat to Suzy. So what do they do? They bring Suzy into the loop and make her look like the hero. Usually Suzy is their direct contact through the process, not Bill. Then Suzy gets to take the options to Bill and say, "Look what I found!" Paul and Steve don't want the praise and glory. They just want to provide a valuable service and get paid.

A PIECE OF THE PIE

As stated earlier, Paul and Steve didn't invent event planning. But they did perfect it. Yet believe it or not, they weren't the first to recognize the opportunity and seize it. Site selection, or the hotel sourcing industry as it's also known, has been around since about the early 1990s when a professional hotelier named Roger Helms recognized the need for client representation, much like a Realtor.

And he was right. Hotels had the event planning market cornered. Think of Suzy coordinating the event for Bill. She needs beds and a conference room for three hundred people for a week. And she also needs meeting spaces for five breakout sessions. Then there are food and beverage, parking, and audiovisual. A hotelier instantly recognizes that Suzy is figuring things out on the fly, so the hotelier says, "Coffee? We can do that. It's $80 a gallon, plus a 22 percent service charge, plus 10 percent tax." To the uninitiated, a hotelier can demand top dollar for all kinds of things and the client is none the wiser.

How many of you reading this know how many cups of coffee you can get out of a gallon, and what's a reasonable price per cup? Roger Helms knew. He knew the industry equation for how many gallons of regular and decaf coffee would be enough for three hundred people. And how much coffee was needed per day, even per break.

He knew how many staff members were needed to help with registration and executing an event with three hundred people. If you hire too many, you are wasting money, while too few staff members can result in unhappy guests because their needs aren't being met.

COFFEE MATH

To figure out how much coffee you need, start out by remembering that a typical gallon of coffee will have twenty cups. Let's say we have a mixed audience of 250 people: 250 x 60 percent who will drink regular coffee = 150 cups = 7.5 gallons of regular coffee, which you will round up to 8 gallons.

Roger knew how much food to order for a lunch buffet for three hundred people. He knew the percentage who were going to not eat a thing, as well as the percentage who would take their meals to their rooms. And he knew the percentage of vegetarians likely to be in attendance.

So Roger Helms pioneered a brand-new industry and launched a company called HelmsBriscoe, and in 2018 he stood as the largest player in the site selection field, contracting $1.4 billion[1] in sales with a 10 percent commission of approximately $140 million. Wait, if he brought in $1.4 billion in sales, how much is that of the total value of the marketplace? *Half a percent.* That's right, the biggest player in the

---

1   Cheryl-Anne Sturken, "HelmsBriscoe Booked a Record $1.42 Billion in Room Revenue in 2018," Northstar Meetings Group, January 8, 2019, https://www.northstarmeetingsgroup.com/News/Independent-Planners/helmsbriscoe-2018-year-end-sales-figures-third-party-planning.

industry has only tapped into less than 0.5 percent of the potential.[2] That leaves more than $328 billion ripe for the picking. And that's where EventPrep comes in.

THE EVENTPREP DIFFERENCE

Today there are four major companies that have wrapped their heads around this opportunity and are seizing their piece of the pie. They created systems and processes for their clients and partners, and they license their name to decentralized contracted sales reps (1099s) who provide services under their brand. So people who want to quit their day job and become an event planner get a business card with the licensed company's name on it, and they use their systems and processes. Most companies follow the industry standard of a 50/50 commission split with the licensee, and they offer limited support.

Roger Helms has one of the largest contracted workforces in the marketplace licensed under his business model, all of them basically salespeople doing hotel sourcing. Imagine more than a thousand Realtors working under one broker, then splitting the commission in half for all the hard work they did individually. And if any of the salespeople leave, all the clients and contacts remain the broker's property.

EventPrep instead follows a franchise model. We want our event planners to take pride in owning their own business. The clients and relationships they make, they get to keep. And *they* reap the majority of the reward for their hard work, not us. In fact, we offer the most

---

2   Michael J. Shapiro, "U.S. Meetings Industry Generates $330 Billion Annually," *Meetings and Conventions, January 9, 2018,* http://www.meetings-conventions.com/News/Industry-Associations/US-Meetings-Industry-Generates-$330-Billion-Annually/.

favorable commission split in the industry and additionally provide a full business model, ongoing support, and client leads.

But does it really work? Is approaching event planning as a franchisee too good to be true? Paul and Steve have actually developed a systematic way to go about penetrating the marketplace. In fact, not long ago one of their new franchisees called Paul and said the process was working so well that he generated an incredible lead. Paul and Steve walked him through the negotiation process, then helped him fill out a proposal. The potential client does 175 events a year, and the timing couldn't have been better because the company was in the process of looking for help with events when the franchisee reached out.

What did our client just do to his business? Half the year is now filled with events. His business has just grown exponentially. He's going to need to hire a full staff, and he's going to make more money than he ever thought possible. Thanks to the EventPrep model, his life just changed forever.

IF THEY'RE GOOD ENOUGH FOR THE PRESIDENT ...

One of Paul and Steve's slogans is: "We save you time, money, and anxiety." This is poignant, given the fact that event planning is actually one of the top ten most stressful jobs in the US.[3] Think about the pressure of being extremely detail oriented, ensuring that every aspect of an event that is important to the client is carried out to the letter. It's an extremely stressful job.

---

3   Sue Hatch, "No Pain, No Gain? Event Planning Ranks High on the Stress List," MeetingsNet, January 12, 2018, https://www.meetingsnet.com/careerlifetravel/no-pain-no-gain-event-planning-ranks-high-stress-list.

But as Paul and Steve have proven, when you have the right systems and processes down, and more importantly when you're prepared, you can pull off the biggest of events gracing the biggest stages in the world … such as former president George W. Bush's first public speaking appearance after he left the White House, the first time he ever appeared publicly as a professionally paid speaker.

The details involved to coordinate that event are about as extreme as it can get. The guys had to navigate the transportation of the former president from Texas to Washington, the security arrangements at every step, and how and where he entered and exited the hotel. They also had to figure out how to get the Marine Corps band there. The Secret Service even had to come through and vet every employee involved as Paul and Steve were setting up. Some 600 guests were expected, and every table had to be set flawlessly. Everything had to be perfect. And it was. And at the end of the night, Bush shook Paul's and Steve's hands and said, "Thanks. It was a great event and I really enjoyed it. See you guys again."

Today the guys use the following tagline: if the president of the United States thinks Paul and Steve are good enough for his event, they'll probably be able to handle yours.

Paul and Steve say all the time that they didn't invent event planning. They just found a way to seize an opportunity and build a better mousetrap—a model that creates a win-win-win for the clients, the hotels, and the event planners. It took years to build what was best for them and their clients, and then fine-tune it so it could be replicated.

And it all started with becoming disruptors.

FRANCHISEE SPOTLIGHT:
ELISA VERTULI

About Elisa:

I grew up on a Christmas tree farm in Ohio. I joined the army after completing ROTC in college, where I met my husband. After four years of active duty, I attended graduate school and received an MA in mathematics. I have held numerous jobs over the years as we moved more than twelve times to various locations across the continental US, Hawaii, and Europe; had two children; and dealt with separation while my husband was attending military schools, deployed for a year to Afghanistan, and many other temporary duty assignments. In addition to my military service, I worked as a pension analyst at an actuarial firm, an adjunct mathematics professor, and a special events coordinator, and I served in many volunteer roles. We currently reside in Omaha, Nebraska. My husband plans to retire from active duty in 2020, when both of our children will be in high school.

Where did you hear about EventPrep?

A friend read about an opportunity with EventPrep and thought I would be a great fit. She also serves in the military and understands the hardship that moving every two to three years has on a career. We have known each other for twenty-seven years, and she knows that I have the drive to work independently, I enjoy working with people from diverse backgrounds, and I often volunteer to plan large events.

What motivated you to become a franchisee?

I was working full time as a special events coordinator for a nonprofit organization because I enjoy planning events that bring people together and make a difference in the community. It was rewarding, but I felt limited by the organization. I like the challenge of thinking outside the box, developing efficient processes, and having autonomy to try my ideas, even if they may seem out of the ordinary to some.

I began a dialogue with Paul after initially speaking with several other employees at EventPrep and Federal Conference. Paul was very easy to talk to, was happy to answer all of my questions, and made time to guide me over the couple of months that it took for me to make my decision. Since both he and Steve were veterans, they had a unique understanding of the challenges I have faced in maintaining a career over the past twenty years. Aside from that, I could tell that they are honest and straightforward as they repeatedly stressed the value of trust within their companies. Even now, they are happy to help anytime I reach out. They clearly love what they do and always manage to make time to guide and develop each franchisee.

What were factors in your decision to become a franchisee?

Aside from seeing the success of Federal Conference, knowing that Paul and Steve would be there to help me succeed was definitely a factor. They continually used the example of learning to ride a bike—that they will be with us until we are ready to go on our own. They even promised guaranteed contracts during the first year. I don't think many other CEOs would promise income to a franchisee, let alone personally guide us as needed.

Another major deciding factor was that there are no geographical boundaries or limitations on growing our business. I only need to own one franchise, but I can do business worldwide. This also means that our family can move as needed and I won't have to start over each time. What an amazing opportunity to own a business that can grow and move with me!

How is your life today as a franchisee?

Aside from the incredible luxury of being able to work on my own schedule, I have also enjoyed learning and using the processes that have been developed. With my background in mathematics, I am logical and thrive on organization and efficiency. The company has created an efficient system that has clearly been a factor in its success, but I have also enjoyed thinking creatively and adding my own ideas to enhance the system.

What is the best part of being a franchisee?

For me, the best part is being in control of my own success and having flexibility to arrange my schedule to best suit my family.

Chapter Four

BECOMING A DISRUPTOR

• • • • • • • • • • • • • • • • • • • •

Clients do not come first. Employees come first. If you take care of your employees, they will take care of the clients.

—SIR RICHARD BRANSON

Picture in your mind how many jewelry stores are in a five-mile radius of wherever you are at this very moment. If you live in a big city like Boston, New York, or Los Angeles, just think about how many jewelry stores surround you. There are at least a handful in every mall. There are a couple in the strip plazas along the way to the mall. Dozens and dozens of jewelry stores, both boutique and chain stores, as far as the eye can see in any given direction. With so many options, how do you choose which one deserves your business?

Before we get to what sets them apart, let's examine what they all have in common. They all claim to be the best in the business. Each store touts its gem quality as superior to competitors'. The fact is, when you peel back the skin of illusion, the gems sitting beneath the glass are actually rated by an outside organization. The diamond earrings at Zales rated a "D" on color and "I1" on clarity technically have the same value as the diamond earrings with a similar clarity and color rating found inside the case at a local boutique jeweler. The same goes for sapphires, emeralds, rubies, and other precious gems. Then what separates one store from another? Perceived value.

Like most women, Paul's wife, Kimberly, really likes jewelry from Tiffany & Co. There's something about that little robin's-egg blue bag. When she sees Paul walking through the door with that bag in hand, she says she knows immediately it's going to be something really good, and she feels special.

Now consider this: the closest Tiffany's to Paul's house is forty-five minutes away in Orlando. But he's going to get into his car and drive by dozens of other jewelry stores all claiming to be the best, who will likely sell the same piece of jewelry for less money. Yet Paul is willing to pay more and drive farther for the perceived value that little blue bag has acquired.

So when Paul and Steve were creating the franchise model of EventPrep, they had Tiffany's in mind. They wanted their business opportunity to stand out above the competition and become that destination store. To do that, they asked themselves a series of questions: How are we going to disrupt the industry? How do we position ourselves in the marketplace so that people will go out of their way to do business with us? How are we going to position ourselves in a marketplace that's already saturated with other jewelry stores—other event planners? How are we going to get them to leave their current event planning company or leave their current employer and buy a franchise?

THE POWER OF INTANGIBLES

Why do people line up at Starbucks and pay upward of $5 for a cup of coffee? Because the person who makes it is called a *barista*. And it's not called a large coffee; it's a *Venti* coffee.

What Starbucks has done, and done brilliantly, is create perceived value. But it's still selling coffee. No matter how many flavors and dashes of this and that you add, your low-fat Venti no-whip iced caramel hazelnut triple-shot macchiato is still coffee. And you'll happily stand in line with a bunch of other people also willing to pay twice as much for coffee.

Harley-Davidson is another great example of a company that has created perceived value. People are so loyal and excited to be associated with that brand that some of them who can't afford to buy a Harley-Davidson motorcycle will still buy the clothing and wear it. They'll get Harley-Davidson tattoos. They live the lifestyle even though they can't buy the main product.

Short of getting EventPrep tattoos, Paul and Steve wanted to inspire that kind of brand loyalty and level of engagement with their business. To stand out in a field of small and large event planning companies, Paul and Steve really had to think about what would make EventPrep different. They could say they cared more about their franchisees, but that's exactly what their competitors would say.

What differentiator would appeal to potential franchisees? After all, this was not a typical sale. If the guys were selling a car, they could show potential customers the car. Buyers could sit in the car, smell the car, touch the car. All their senses would get stroked. But when you're talking to someone about a vision, an opportunity, you are selling them an intangible—essentially a dream. Paul and Steve needed to get potential franchisees to buy into their vision, to put themselves in the driver's seat without really seeing, smelling, or touching the car.

Ultimately, the underpinnings of their success would come down to three things: compensation, ownership stake, and bridging the financial gap.

A BETTER COMPENSATION MODEL

The guys knew that all of their event planning competitors would claim they cared the most about their people. So they asked themselves: Is it possible to actually care *more* than the others? Can we put our money where our mouth is?

First and foremost, the reality is that businesses exist to make money. So it's no surprise that increasing profits is a major driving force for a lot of business owners. And, understandably so, growth and increased profits drove Paul and Steve early on in their event planning endeavors. More money meant more opportunities both personally and professionally. Over time, success became more about building something that they would be proud to wake up and go off to lead. They wanted to build a culture of energetic, dedicated, passionate individuals who loved what they did for a living. Paul and Steve wanted to create something bigger than themselves. And before long, their business model was getting attention.

Competitors with a polar opposite 1099 business model (i.e., subcontractors) suddenly sat up and took notice. These companies basically hire anyone and everyone who has a modicum of sales ability, furnish them business cards, and then tell them to sell, sell, sell, with 50 percent of the profits going back to the company. As subcontractors, they receive no benefits, and they lack the cohesive environment that is traditionally associated with a winning culture. These companies saw an upstart event planning company actually putting its franchisees and W-2 employees first, taking exceptional care of them, and not being greedy.

And that philosophy became a cornerstone for EventPrep.

When most every firm in the industry is splitting revenues 50/50 with their sales representatives for every dollar that comes in, Paul and Steve decided on 70/30. Franchisees get 70 percent, while the guys get 30 percent. Why would they take such a smaller cut than the rest of the industry? Because they realized that their job as a franchisor is to help people start and grow a business. Paul and Steve's job is to make franchisees successful. If their franchisees go out there and spin their wheels and make zero money, the guys make zero return on their investment. It's all about unit-level economics.

Paul and Steve knew that they would only be successful when their franchisees were successful. Allowing franchisees the larger share of the pie would ensure that kind of success.

OWNERSHIP STAKE

As explained previously, many of Paul and Steve's competitors operate under a 1099 model, which means their people are basically subcontractors/licensees, doing business under the company flag. At any time the licensee could walk away, be fired, or be pushed away, and they are left with nothing but a memory and another bullet on their résumé. With EventPrep, franchisees are in business for themselves. *They* own the business. The clients that franchisees bring to the table remain *their* clients.

Paul and Steve knew that to be a disruptor in the industry, they had to get radical. They had to care more about their franchisees than profits. So the second franchisees sign on with EventPrep, they start working and building something for themselves. And the guys are right there beside them, helping those franchisees build it. Whether the franchisee puts in six years or sixteen, at the end of the day they have something that they've built, something that has actual value, and something they can sell to monetize their exit. They are building a nest egg and have something to show for all the hard work. Unlike their competitors, Paul and Steve's model allows franchisees to build equity in themselves.

> **WITH EVENTPREP, FRANCHISEES ARE IN BUSINESS FOR THEMSELVES. *THEY* OWN THE BUSINESS. THE CLIENTS THAT FRANCHISEES BRING TO THE TABLE REMAIN *THEIR* CLIENTS.**

And if and when a franchisee wants to get out of the event planning business, Paul and Steve assess the franchise's value and have right of first refusal to buy it. Or perhaps another franchisee may be interested in buying a colleague's business. Either way, there's an exit strategy available that benefits everyone.

Disrupting the industry with their ownership model, Paul and Steve have created something that *no one else is doing.*

BRIDGING THE GAP

When Paul and Steve's competitors bring someone on board, those licensees may not get paid for six, nine, or sometimes twelve months. Why is that? Because the first event a licensee might sell, the first client they land, likely will be planning for an event as far as twelve months in advance. That means the licensee is going to have to wait just as long to get paid … with half going back to the company they work for.

For most of us, that's a huge gap. How many of us are in a financial position to wait that long? Well, that gap is something that Paul and Steve looked at … and figured out a brilliant way to address: the Quick Start Program.

All business owners want to attract their own customers. Because of the success of their other business, Federal Conference, which plans and delivers three thousand events a year, Paul and Steve realized they could take the fruit off that vine and allow the new franchisees to work with established clients. This unique model creates immediate income for franchisees while they build their own clientele, instead of having to wait six months to a year for a paycheck. For the first twelve months, the Quick Start Program bridges the financial gap. But it took a little tweaking.

THIS UNIQUE MODEL CREATES IMMEDIATE INCOME FOR FRANCHISEES WHILE THEY BUILD THEIR OWN CLIENTELE, INSTEAD OF HAVING TO WAIT SIX MONTHS TO A YEAR FOR A PAYCHECK.

The first two franchisees Paul and Steve ever brought on board, Jason and Lynn, flew to Northern Virginia to the EventPrep training center. The guys trained their new franchisees for a little over a week, and were understandably excited to make sure Jason and Lynn were successful in their new businesses.

So the guys plucked some ripe fruit from Federal Conference, forty events for each franchisee, to bridge the gap as they built their own client lists. Mind you, these Federal Conference clients were ready to go and expecting professional event planners to pull off their events. Immediately the new franchisees balked. Way too many events for emerging business owners! But clearly the heart and intent were there, and over time Paul and Steve figured out the right formula with the proper number of events to help bridge the financial gap.

It is a true win-win model, because Paul and Steve's clients are being taken care of and the franchisees have cash flow while learning how to run their business. If they started out on their own, everything would be a matter of trial and error. The new business comes with new technology, new procedures, and new paperwork, and the program allows franchisees to practice and learn how to build their business, all while earning money.

WHAT IS THE QUICK START PROGRAM?

For the first twelve months of operations, EventPrep provides new franchisees with immediate access to corporate and government events to service for the purpose of generating accelerated revenues and bridge the financial gap within this initial startup period. Additionally, the Quick Start Program provides new franchisees with the opportunity to practice the skills they learned in training, become proficient with the associated software programs, and establish and grow their own industry relationships.

DISRUPTING THE INDUSTRY STATUS QUO

With today's marketing and analytics, you can see everything. You can determine when someone has opened your email, you know when someone clicked on your ad, you know when someone shared something on LinkedIn or Facebook. The analytics can be frightening ... and amusing.

When Paul and Steve launch new marketing materials for their company, they are very careful and calculated. And like clockwork, they sit and watch the analytics. They get a daily report from LinkedIn, for example, that says 875 people viewed that particular ad that particular day. They can see how many people, from which industry, from which company, even what positions they held in the company.

Every time the guys post something new, their competitors are the first ones to click to see what the guys are up to. And it's not just the salespeople—it's the entire organization all the way up to the C-suite. It's almost like throwing a grenade and waiting for it to tick off and blow up. The guys hit send, launch it, and then they count down. Why are their competitors so preoccupied with what Paul and Steve are doing? After all, there are other event planners out there besides them.

For Paul and Steve, people aren't numbers. People are the *culture.* And that is why they are leaving their competitors to work with Paul and Steve. The COO of one of their biggest competitors called and admitted, "We're not too concerned about you stealing our customers; we're more worried about our people leaving us."

The competition is interested in what Paul and Steve are doing, and how they're doing it ... all over the world, from Japan to Korea, to Italy, Germany, and the UK.

CULTURE OF SUCCESS

A better compensation model. The ability to truly own your own business instead of working for someone else. The Quick Start Program to provide immediate revenue to bridge the financial gap. These three differentiators are part of the guys' larger culture of success. Paul and Steve also generate leads for their franchisees. They invest in advertising and help them build their business, which is something their competitors don't seem to do.

What they created with EventPrep, in essence, is a culture built on relationships. It makes sense, because hotel selection is a very relationship-driven field. One of their franchisees, a minister, says the deciding factor for him to purchase an EventPrep franchise was a customer of Paul and Steve's who couldn't say enough nice things about the guys.

WHAT THEY CREATED WITH EVENTPREP, IN ESSENCE, IS A CULTURE BUILT ON RELATIONSHIPS.

The customer knew her minister friend was thinking about changing careers and recommended he speak with Paul and Steve about the EventPrep opportunity. One of the first things he asked was if he could speak with other franchisees. They provided him with a list of all their franchisees. Later, the minister said to Paul and Steve, "Through the entire experience I felt like you didn't care about you, you only cared about me. What nailed it for me was talking to your franchisees. At the end of the day, every one of your franchisees said they weren't necessarily making a million dollars yet, but they're in the right place. They felt supported, and they trust the people they are doing business with.

Everything Paul and Steve have ever said they're going to do for me, they've done ... and then some!"

Culture is so subjective. There's no way to measure whether it's good or bad. But from Paul and Steve's perspective, what your people say about you, unprompted and unedited, defines a culture of success. And just like the old adage about being judged by those whose company you keep, the employees within a company reflect the owners, and ultimately the corporate culture, of the business.

That's why creating the right culture is crucial in not only attracting, but retaining, the right talent.

FRANCHISEE SPOTLIGHT: BROOKLYN CARTWRIGHT

About Brooklyn:

I am twenty-four years old, born and raised in Dayton, Ohio. I moved to Atlanta, Georgia, when I was in middle school. I graduated from the Georgia Southern University with a degree in sport management with an emphasis in business. Prior to EventPrep, I was a college basketball coach for three years, making stops at Lenoir-Rhyne University, Marshall University, and South Carolina State University.

Where did you hear about EventPrep?

Steve's daughter Maggie is my best friend of almost seven years. We were in Steve's pool one summer day and out of nowhere I just started asking him questions about what he did. I always knew he was the president of a company, but I never had a real idea about what he did. So my curious mind just asked. Before you knew it, we had talked for probably an hour or so about what he did at EventPrep and how he and Paul had started franchising a year prior. That conversation was the first of many.

What motivated you to become a franchisee?

At the time, I was a college basketball coach. I was working seventy-hour weeks and missing holidays with my family, which began to take somewhat of a toll. Don't get me wrong, I *love* basketball and coaching, and hope to get involved again someday, but the time constraints became a real challenge. I was living in Orangeburg, South Carolina, at the time—basically the middle of nowhere—and prior to that I lived in West Virginia, which is also kind of nowhere (no offense, West Virginia—I had a nice time there). I was a twenty-four-year-old with zero social life, living in towns that I disliked, chasing a "job." Needless to say, I had been thinking about making a change, but was somewhat scared and had no idea what I would even do if I decided to get out of coaching. Coaching basketball was all I had ever done at that point. It was almost a subconscious thing when I started asking Steve those questions in the pool. I didn't even realize I was grilling him. After that conversation I went home, and I couldn't stop thinking about it. I called my grandmother and my mother, my two most trusted advisers, and brought up the idea to them. I thought about it every day for a week straight before I finally decided to give Steve a call.

The funny thing is, I had actually met Paul's entire immediate family before I ever met him—all three of his kids and his wife. Even his dog, Moose. Kind of funny to think about now. Steve has essentially been my second father since 2012. I've spent countless weekends at his house and even went on vacation with him, Maggie, Brendan (Paul's son), and their family. I have had nothing but good experiences with them. From the moment I began talking with them from a business perspective, I knew that I would be in good hands if they were crazy enough to take a chance on me, an industry outsider with zero experience. They are really good people, they hire good people, and they surround themselves with good people. It has been such a blessing to know the two of them.

What were factors in your decision to become a franchisee?

The major factors were how much of a quality of life I would get back, the fact that I trusted Steve and Paul, and that I could really see myself being successful doing this.

How is your life today as a franchisee?

It's great! Just getting started and really getting myself out there has been fun. I'm somewhat of a hustler by nature, so I really enjoy the grind of making connections and seeking out new business. I love to talk to and meet people, so this is definitely in my lane. I've moved back home to Atlanta and already connected with some great friends.

I'm really enjoying this new life.

What is the best part of being a franchisee?

The freedom and support. I get to wake up every day and decide what I want to do that day and how I want to spend the rest of my life. Something about that is simply *freeing*. I love meeting new people and I love *helping* people, so I am ecstatic to be in a field in which I still get to serve others. If I wasn't serving people in some capacity, I would be miserable. I am most excited to be able to give back to the women's basketball community, which has given so much to me. The best part about being a franchisee is that I get to choose my own destiny.

Chapter Five

ATTRACTING TALENT

• • • • • • • • • • • • • • • • • • • •

It's more important to hire people with the right
qualities than with specific experience.

—J. WILLARD MARRIOTT

Steve can read them like a book.

His thirty-plus-year career in law enforcement as a detective and undercover agent, along with his military career as a criminal investigator, has made him an expert at reading people. On several occasions, Steve has gone undercover to buy drugs or pick up a prostitute, which ultimately ended poorly for the guilty parties. At any time during his undercover work, one small mistake on Steve's part could have been dangerous, if not deadly, so he not only had to be aware of what the perpetrator was saying, but their body language as well. It's funny how most of the bad guys still claimed to be innocent, even after being caught in the act.

No one is likely to end up in jail or hurt when participating in a job interview or applying to buy a franchise, but many of the people skills Steve acquired on the street with the bad guys have helped him to master the art of recognizing the good guys when onboarding new talent.

Traditionally, there are two roles being played during a job interview: the applicant and the interviewer. Applicants are selling themselves to get in, and interviewers are acting as gatekeepers. During this process, words can come out of an applicant's mouth that conflict with what body language is saying. Résumés can exaggerate only the good things a person wants you to know about his or her experience, as well as a wish list of the qualities a person would like to have. People won't openly tell you the bad things, so how do you filter through what is real and what is merely an illusion?

Steve's innate ability to read people has served him well in the past, but he's also keenly aware of the need to maintain strict discipline and follow established hiring processes when screening and onboarding potential talent.

For a business owner, hiring people is very much like investing. There are as many investment opportunities out there as there are job applicants, and every one of them is screaming, "I'm the best!" On the surface, many will be tempting. But you probably shouldn't just say yes to the first good thing that comes along, at least not without examining it closely beforehand. We've all heard the saying: "If it sounds too good to be true, it probably is."

Jack Daly, a mentor friend of Steve and Paul, once advised them to *hire slowly and fire quickly.* It's a practice Steve and Paul still exercise to this day. Filling an open position shouldn't be just another task checked off the hiring manager's checklist. Recruiting is not a hiring event, but rather a slow and strategic process.

As you will read in this chapter, Paul met Jason in 2003 and courted him for thirteen years before Jason finally left his job and joined Paul and Steve as their first franchisee with EventPrep. How many phone calls, emails, personal cards, dinners, etc. occurred over the years before Jason said yes? People often tend to rush to the urgent at the cost of the important, and hiring managers are no exception. Take your time—it's not a race.

So, before you offer someone a job, do research, check references, and ask many questions. Do people you are considering have the right qualifications and skill sets to perform the job? The right attitude and motivation to succeed? Would they be a good fit with your existing culture? Do candidates' social media pages reflect what they said during the interview?

Do you have a system or a process to onboard new talent? Do you wait until you have a vacancy or need to hire, or do you build an organizational chart of the company you want to become with several vacant seats and start identifying potential candidates now, and then court them for several months or years with the end game in mind? If you were hiring a salesperson, wouldn't it be better to identify the top players in your industry and recruit them (no matter how long it takes) instead of weeding through the applicants that were cut from the other team because they weren't good enough, and now need another job?

Again, it all goes back to preparation.

THE LINK BETWEEN HR AND INVESTIGATIVE WORK

At first glance, it would seem that human resources and police work have very little in common. After all, when we think about police work, we think of protecting the public, maintaining order, taking down the bad guys, and interrogation. Interrogating a suspect is a valuable skill in police work. Justifiably so, it comes across as scary. You're likely picturing a single bright light swinging in a smoke-filled, dingy room. Someone is sitting in the hot seat, sweating profusely, while an investigator grills the person with questions, trying to get him or her to crack.

But when we step back a moment, we can see that interrogations are nothing more than a series of questions designed to get to the truth, to allow an investigator to see the whole picture and provide insight into the mind of the interview subject. This is where the link between police work and an HR director's job becomes clearer. Both formal and informal interviews include a lot of probing and questioning of a job applicant.

Effective interviewing requires a unique skill set in the realm of communication, an ability to read others' body language, the capacity to process the verbal information as well as the nonverbal information, and the knowledge of what types of questions to ask to get the interviewee to open up and provide the answers you seek.

This is a skill Steve honed not just in his police work, but as a special agent with the Army Criminal Investigations Division (CID). He used his prowess and training in body language interpretation and deception identification while in Iraq to interview soldiers, officers, Department of Defense employees, and Iraqi civilians, among others. Even when Steve had an interpreter telling him what the suspect was saying, he was busy watching body language. The interpreter could always repeat what the suspect was saying, but with body language, Steve knew he only had one opportunity.

He had to be extremely observant of behaviors to gain insight, and an advantage, in the dialogue. Things like eye movement, breathing patterns, and hand gestures all told a story that either verified or contradicted what the suspect was saying.

From their experience in law enforcement, Paul and Steve knew that reading, understanding, and giving people what they needed to make them feel at ease would aid them in interviewing potential candidates ... and ultimately lead to success at attracting and retaining the right talent.

ENABLING THEM TO BECOME

For their first ten years in business together, Steve played the primary role in interviewing talent. And at the time of this writing, the majority of those people are still with the company. But when it came to *retaining* talent, and especially with the launch of EventPrep franchises, Paul's background in recruiting and sales really came into play. Going back to his days working as a recruiter for the National Guard, Paul didn't see recruiting as an event, but a process.

If you've seen the movie *The Sixth Sense,* you're familiar with the line from Haley Joel Osment's character describing his unique psychic ability to spot ghosts: "I see dead people." Paul's version of that unique ability while serving as a recruiter can be summed up with an equally compelling, though less creepy line: "I see enlistments." Recognizing talent and opportunity in potential candidates was almost a sixth sense to him. Whether he happened to be talking to people in church, at the gym, at work, at the library, or on a sports field, Paul was always looking, listening, assessing, and asking questions. Why? Because he is passionate about people, about helping them find their purpose, and he only sells what he believes in. As Mark Twain once said, "The two most important days in your life are the day you are born and the day you find out why."

There's a stigma about military recruiters that is worth mentioning here. Specifically, that they are like used car salespeople, telling young people anything they want to hear just to get them to sign up.

HE IS PASSION-ATE ABOUT PEOPLE, ABOUT HELPING THEM FIND THEIR PURPOSE, AND HE ONLY SELLS WHAT HE BELIEVES IN.

But Paul approached the job with a sincere interest in the lives of the young men and women whose paths he crossed. One young man in particular told Paul he wanted to be a lawyer, not sign up for military service.

Paul knew he didn't have any enlistment programs that went from high school to law school. But he also knew that the National Guard could be a stepping-stone to get to law school. After all, the National Guard is a community within a community. Everything that any other community has, the military has, from plumbers to accountants to psychologists. Any civilian job you can think of has a counterpart in the military, because it has to be self-sufficient in times of natural disaster, civil unrest, and war.

That means that the military has lawyers as well. Lawyers who do everything from environmental law to criminal defense to estate planning. Part of Paul's process was to learn more about the person, so he asked the high school senior some questions: What kind of law do you want to practice? Have you talked with any lawyers? Have you ever been in a courtroom?

It turned out that the teenager loved the idealized image of being a lawyer—nice salary, nice car, wining and dining with movers and shakers, high-stakes courtroom drama—yet he had never set foot in a courtroom. So Paul met with his guidance counselor and his parents, and scheduled a field trip to the local courthouse. Paul was in uniform and the young man dressed appropriately, and the two spent a day in traffic/misdemeanor court. With Paul's background in law enforcement and administrative justice, he was able to quietly explain the proceedings and the roles of the players in the courtroom.

About halfway through the morning the judge realized he had a serviceman in the room and asked Paul if he had business with the court. Paul stood up, identified himself not as a recruiter but a career counselor with the National Guard, and introduced the young man as someone with a desire to work in the legal system. Not only did the judge take the time to stop the court to meet the young man, but he invited them to join him for lunch.

Paul never directly tried to recruit the high school senior. Instead he allowed him to learn more about himself and his passion. Ronald O. Harrison, a two-star general and mentor to Paul, once told him, "Paul, go find young people of promise and enable them to become."

Recruiting for Paul means finding people who have dreams and helping them fulfill those dreams. Paul eventually put the young man into a job as a legal clerk in the military, where he was handling legal documents, working side by side with lawyers, and researching legal case law.

He doesn't know if that teenager ever became a lawyer. What was important, however, was that Paul enabled him to become.

PREPARING FOR BLIND OPPORTUNITIES

On its most basic level, recruiting is about connecting people with their passion, their purpose. The funny thing is that sometimes we are aware of our purpose and sometimes it takes a little outside help. And sometimes when you think you are preparing for one thing, you don't actually realize you are preparing for something that hasn't yet been revealed to you.

> **SOMETIMES WHEN YOU THINK YOU ARE PREPARING FOR ONE THING, YOU DON'T ACTUALLY REALIZE YOU ARE PREPARING FOR SOMETHING THAT HASN'T YET BEEN REVEALED TO YOU.**

Case in point: one of Paul and Steve's top-producing franchisees, Jason, didn't realize that over a decade of hard work as a former hotelier was preparing him to triple his salary and live a life he'd always dreamed of but thought was out of reach.

Jason resided in Hollywood, Florida, and worked twelve-plus hours a day for a Hilton in Fort Lauderdale. Always in a suit and tie, he spent all of his time commuting, hustling, selling, and making deliveries on-site. If he had a customer with an event on the property, he was there until the customer left, which often could be as late as two in the morning. That was his reality, spending more time at the hotel than with his family.

Paul met Jason in 2003 while serving as the recruiting chief for the Army National Guard. Paul was in charge of a large event being held at Jason's hotel for a group of more than a thousand people. Jason had been assigned to Paul as the contact to make sure everything with the event ran smoothly. Paul immediately saw that Jason was a natural at his job and the two hit it off. He found out about Paul's affinity for Heineken and would meet him at the end of each day with a couple of ice-cold beers so the guys could relax and discuss the details for the following day. Even after the event was long over, Paul tapped Jason once in a while for his professional opinion when dealing with other hoteliers. Jason became an advocate for Paul, and would do industry favors to help make sure Paul was getting the best deal.

So, naturally, when Paul and Steve launched Federal Conference in 2006, Jason was one of the first people Paul tried to recruit. The timing, however, just wasn't right. With a family to support, Jason needed security like insurance and a savings plan, something the guys simply weren't in a position to provide in the early years. The years wore on and every time Paul and Steve landed a big contract, Paul would offer Jason an opportunity to come work for them. And every time, the timing wasn't right. Perhaps it was a case of staying where he was comfortable, even though it wasn't the best option, rather than taking a chance.

But over time Jason witnessed Paul and Steve's successes. He saw them making a name for themselves in the industry, doing thousands of events, and hiring dozens of new staff members. All of a sudden, Paul and Steve offered insurance. All of a sudden, they had a 401(k).

So Paul reached out to Jason in 2016 about an opportunity called EventPrep. Jason happened to be sitting in traffic, commuting home from work, when Paul called. This time was finally the right time. "I have passed up way too many opportunities to work with you. And I've passed up far too many success stories. I've watched you just knock it out of the park every time. I am not going to let this one get by me. I love the idea of it. I trust you. Let's do it." Jason quit his job and joined Paul and Steve at last.

In his first year he contracted more than a quarter of a million dollars for himself, three times what he was making with Hilton. But it wasn't the money that had swayed Jason. It wasn't the benefits. Paul couldn't have taken him to enough concerts or ball games or buy him enough dinners to make him leave his other job. In the end, Jason had to realize he needed a new life.

Today he not only has his own business, but he has that new life. He moved to North Florida and now has a house with a pool. He spends every day with his son. He actually gets up, takes him to school, and picks him up after school. He not only gets to bring him to baseball practice—Jason became the coach of his son's Little League team.

JASON'S UNSOLICITED EMAIL TO PAUL AND STEVE

Gentlemen,

EventPrep is good, but you two are better. Thank you from the bottom of my heart for the opportunity you both laid in front of me. You took me out of my passionless work life and gave me a new outlook and perspective on work and life. But most importantly, you gave me my family back. I tell everyone I speak to about the two of you and what amazing people you are. Forgetting everything else, just honest, good, amazing people. Things just took a very exciting and possibly positively drastic turn for my business, which will change my life in many ways, and I owe that to you two for putting me in that position.

RETAINING TALENT

A business's success is not just based on attracting and recruiting the right talent. It's also about *retaining the talent.*

This is a lesson Paul learned early in life while serving in the military. While in attendance at a conference on recruiting, one of the leaders in the field took the stage, a towering man from Georgia, six foot seven, with a thick southern drawl. Yet instead of talking about recruiting, he began educating the audience about the importance of *retaining* people.

He explained that it is cheaper sometimes to try to retain the good soldiers the military already has than it is to go out and replace them with new recruits. To illustrate, he picked up a state-of-the-art (for the time) IBM Selectric III typewriter, a relatively expensive piece of government equipment, held it up over his head like Moses holding the tablets, and smashed it on the floor. Gasps ripple through the room.

Then he said, "Y'all are worried about a typewriter that cost a couple hundred dollars. Do you know what it costs to enlist someone in the military? It's $18,000 from contact to contract. That does not include his training. When he's at basic training, that's another $200,000. Yet we let soldiers walk out the front door every day. We let them walk out and get a job as a civilian or go off to college and wish them luck instead of working on how to retain that talent and investment. We care more about wasting a $200 typewriter than a $200,000 soldier."

Just as important as recruiting the right talent, business owners and leaders need to make the environment attractive to retain the right talent.

Using Jason once again as our example, Steve and Paul knew he had taken a big chance when he signed the agreement. He had quit his job and was risking the security of his family to join EventPrep. Did Paul send him a bunch of manuals to read? No, he sent a $200 basket with wine, cheese, and sweets to Jason's wife, Vicki, with a note that let her know how happy the guys were that they were joining the EventPrep family. Paul and Steve wanted Jason and Vicki to take a moment to celebrate.

IF RECRUITING IS ABOUT EMPOWERING, RETAINING IS ABOUT CELEBRATING— SHOWING GRATITUDE AND APPRECIATION.

If recruiting is about empowering, retaining is about celebrating—showing gratitude and appreciation. Keeping people happy and encouraging them to want to stay isn't magic. Business owners should celebrate the new people coming on board, and include their families. You want people to want to come to work. You want people who want to work in the environment that you're creating. But how do you create that kind of environment?

By establishing the right culture.

FRANCHISEE SPOTLIGHT: JASON HOROWITZ

About Jason:

I was born in Birmingham, Alabama at a time when people were still not very accepting. The KKK approached my father one day, and as a Jewish family, that was scary, but they offered him membership because of his skin color. That sparked our move to Florida when I was two, and subsequently I grew up in South Florida. I met my wife at Florida International University, where I earned a BS in hospitality management. I started my career as a front desk agent in a hotel that no longer exists. From there I held positions of manager on duty, sous chef, front desk manager, and restaurant manager. I then landed my first convention management position and continued to climb the ranks from convention services manager to director of catering, working for major hotel brands as well as Disney. After my son was born in 2009, both my personal life and professional life started to shift focus. My passion for family began to grow and my passion for extremely strenuous, long hours began to shrink. Toward the end of my hotel career, I had a real need to change my lifestyle as I thought my health and family were deteriorating. When Paul and Steve came knocking, it was the perfect time for me to make a change.

Where did you hear about EventPrep?

I met Paul and Steve about fourteen years ago. I was the event manager assigned to a group of about eight hundred recruiting specialists in the National Guard that Paul was the contact for. During the conference, Paul and Steve approached me about executing something for them. Long story short, I made it happen, the event was a huge success, the three of us bonded, and now we are here. In between the event and now, Paul and I kept in touch to find a way to work together. It never happened, other than a couple of consulting jobs I did for them while they built Federal Conference. The main reason was that every time he had something for me, I had been promoted or received a raise, so it just didn't work out. But over that time, I learned more about Paul the person, not the businessman. More importantly, so did my wife. Paul called me one day and said, "Jason, I have a great idea. We are finally going to work together and I don't have to pay you!" Who wouldn't jump on that, right? So we spoke about it, he made me an offer to build my own franchise and gave me the security I needed to make a change. Because my wife understood the type of people Paul and Steve were, she agreed, and franchise number one was established.

What motivated you to become a franchisee?

I had maxed out on physical and emotional stress levels in the event management world. Fourteen-hour days, six days a week became the norm. I truly was at the top of the industry when looking at people in my position, but I was drained and ready for a change. I was always stressed out and rarely saw my child. I am surprised he even knew who I was for the first six years of his life.

Paul and Steve are just about the best people you could hope to know. They are honest, full of integrity, faithful, loving, driven, focused, fair ... I could go on and on. I have so many adjectives I can use to describe them, and they are truly like extended family to me. I worked with them once, stayed in touch for years, and now I have the opportunity to build something huge with them. They have changed my life. When these guys say they are going to do something, they do it. I joked with Paul years ago when he offered me this opportunity and said that I missed the boat once, but I'm not going to again. They truly help people and care about them.

What were factors in your decision to become a franchisee?

The biggest factors included the lifestyle change—and really, Paul and Steve.

How is your life today as a franchisee?

It's a completely different world. I wake up and get to take my son to school almost every day now. I get to participate in school and life events and really be a part of his life. I missed out on so much when he was a baby. Fortunately he saved the milestones for when I was actually around, but I still missed too much. I go to work in my pajamas while I sip on my coffee and no one disturbs me, except my dog. I make my own schedule, vacation when I want to, and answer to no one. I am valued by Paul and Steve and love being a part of building the business and helping new franchisees. I get to travel to so many places now for conferences and sites, and I get spoiled along the way (never a bad thing), where I used to be the one spoiling my clients. In short, my life has done a 180-degree turn, and I could not be happier.

What is the best part of being a franchisee?

My life changed from being an overworked, under-appreciated employee to being a self-employed business owner.

Chapter Six

ESTABLISHING A CULTURE

· ·

If you are lucky enough to be someone's employer, then you have a moral obligation to make sure people do look forward to coming to work in the morning.

—JOHN MACKEY, WHOLE FOODS MARKET

What would you do if suddenly you had an extra $1,000, but had to give it away?

Paul and Steve gave each of their fifty employees a chance to answer that exact question following a profitable year for Federal Conference in 2012. The guys, of course, wanted the business to make money, but they realized they also had a responsibility to give back to the community. Up until that point, Paul and Steve had their own personal gifting strategies for their respective households, but as a business they hadn't developed a formal strategy.

After looking at the numbers and discussing it, the guys came up with a figure of $50,000 to give to charity. But which one, with so many to choose from? Cancer had left a significant footprint in the lives of Steve and his family, and Steve himself was a cancer survivor. It would have been very easy and appropriate for the guys to simply write a $50,000 check to the American Cancer Society and be done with it.

But Paul and Steve knew that this opportunity was bigger than the two of them. So they began to consider: "Because our employees are central to our success, how do we include them in the decision and allow them to participate in the joy of giving?"

They knew if they rallied everyone together to hash out the best charity to donate the money to, it would create havoc ... and likely resentment. But how could they fairly let everyone have a piece of it? Then the proverbial light bulb came on: fifty employees ... $50,000. Everyone would get $1,000 to donate to a charity of their choice. The only rule was it had to be a bona fide 50l(c)(3), recognized by the federal government as a not-for-profit organization.

So the guys assembled everyone for their usual Monday morning company meeting and explained the concept. Suddenly, eyes were glowing. The employees were looking at each other, then looking back at Paul and Steve. "Each one of you is going to have $1,000 to give away to something that you hold near and dear to your heart. Something that's important to you," repeated the guys.

Lots of chatter and questions followed, and Paul and Steve gave them the forms to fill out and the deadlines for submission. The entire building was buzzing with happiness and positivity. Employees were discussing which charity they would give to, and some who happened to be passionate about the same cause pooled their money to present a larger check. One employee told a story of how the Shriners Hospitals had helped her little brother after he had been badly burned as a child and almost died. She had always wanted to give back somehow, but never had the means. Until now.

The employees were learning about each other on levels never experienced before. There was sincere compassion and appreciation, and in the communication a positive culture was emerging. Suddenly people were talking about things that were important to them. Senior, salaried staff and $10-an-hour workers were connecting. For those workers in the trenches, the lifeblood of the organization, that very well may have been their first job. Maybe they were in college and had been hired to answer a phone or file paperwork. They had never been faced with an opportunity to give away $1,000. Many didn't even know how to comprehend it at first and had no idea what was important to them ... because they had never been forced to think about it.

Now they had to start doing a personal inventory. They talked to their families, parents, and friends. They felt like they had an awesome responsibility on their shoulders, because they had the chance to make an impact.

So did the guys just put the checks in a stack of envelopes with a letter of explanation and mail them off? Not by a long shot. Paul and Steve own an event planning company, so they decided to make it the event to end all events. They rented out a yacht club in Northern Virginia and sent out formal invitations to all fifty of the recipients. At the event, Paul and Steve called each employee and recipient up, one at a time, then awarded the check, offered handshakes, and took pictures. The media and the local politicians came. It had become a community event.

That one decision to allow their employees to own the giving connected Paul and Steve to their team. It connected the employees to the community. That model wasn't in their business plan. It was in their hearts.

And that is where the culture of a business can live or die.

BY DEFAULT OR BY DESIGN

There are two facts about a business's culture: (1) it will define itself either by default or by design, and (2) it is created at the top and cascades downward.

THERE ARE TWO FACTS ABOUT A BUSINESS'S CULTURE: (1) IT WILL DEFINE ITSELF EITHER BY DEFAULT OR BY DESIGN, AND (2) IT IS CREATED AT THE TOP AND CASCADES DOWNWARD.

Fortunately, the basis for Paul and Steve's relationship is faith. Their belief binds them, informs their decisions, and defines their values and ethics. They are very different men, but their commonality is their faith and a unique, unconditional love and respect that they have for one another. And they both realize that it takes great effort and dedication to build a beautiful, healthy culture—and next to nothing to rip it apart. When leadership doesn't address or rectify one small incident, that culture can sour overnight.

By design, Paul and Steve work hard to maintain the culture. They reflect on it daily and are constantly taking its temperature. If for any reason Paul or Steve ever see or sense that something just isn't quite right, they address it immediately. Their primary focus is making sure their employees are happy, safe, respected, and making a competitive wage.

In fact, the bottom of the policy manual that every employee gets has written in big, black, bold letters: "If we get it right with you, you'll get it right with the customer."

INVESTING IN PEOPLE

In Paul and Steve's headquarters to this day are many of the original employees. Tina Marie started as an event planner, ended up being a manager, went over to registration, and finally became the senior registration manager. She's been on the employee recognition board for just about every category more than anyone else because she's a rock star in everything that she does. But why that kind of overachieving? Because Paul and Steve invest in their employees. Tina Marie has seen true compassion and heart when she needed it most.

For example, when Tina's sister passed away, Paul took the day off of work to make the four-hour drive to attend the funeral. He didn't know her sister or anyone else there, for that matter, but he came so he could walk up to Tina Marie, hug her, offer her words of comfort, and pay his respects. The guys have attended dozens of wedding showers, baby showers, housewarmings, and even US citizenship ceremonies, because they consider their employees family.

Steve and Paul may have put the culture in motion, but the employees have embraced it and owned it, and now it's taken on a life of its own. For the employees, it's *their* culture, it's *their* company. Paul and Steve don't organize these Halloween events, or the chili cookoffs, or the Thanksgiving Day potlucks, or the ongoing fundraisers. The employees do.

For a Halloween party at the headquarters, several of the staff members dressed up like patients, nurses, and doctors in a demented insane asylum. They actually went all out and decorated their whole section to look like a hospital ward.

It's pretty simple, really. These folks that Paul and Steve have brought on board are going to spend significant time with their work family, so why wouldn't they want it to be a cool place? Why wouldn't they want it to be fun? Why wouldn't they want it to be the most productive they could possibly make it?

FEELING APPRECIATED

Recognizing employees is a key element for maintaining culture. Paul and Steve have created various internal awards to acknowledge exceptional work. But they do much more than just say, "Hey, thanks, here's a certificate." Instead, they give the employee some type of monetary gift, $250 or $500, a nice bonus to take the family out to dinner and maybe go buy a little something special they might not have spent their own money on.

But back in 2012, when Paul and Steve were initially considering what kinds of rewards they wanted to give, they looked at the demographics of their employees to come up with the best fit. It's just the nature of the event planning business, but the majority of their employees happened to be female. The guys realized they had wives, moms, single moms, professional women—and they wanted to recognize all those workhorses who were taking folders home at night and working until 10:00 p.m., the people sacrificing family time because they took pride in their work and in the business.

Because the job often cuts into employees' personal lives, the guys wanted to do what they could to take the sting out of that. So they decided the most creative solution would be if people named employee of the quarter had a cleaning service for their homes for the entire next quarter.

It seemed like an ideal solution. Paul and Steve made it policy, negotiated a price, and secured a cleaning company. When they announced it, the building was abuzz. Everyone was thrilled about the prospect of not having to clean the house after a long day of work.

But at the end of the day, when they gave employees a choice of either three months of cleaning services or a cash equivalent option, 100 percent took the cash. Not one person took the cleaning service.

As the saying goes, the guys found out that "cash is king."

HAMILTONS FOR HAMILTON

Paul and Steve like giving cash away, but they are more *experience* kind of guys. Even with Paul's personal life, he'd rather take his wife to California, go backstage to watch her favorite show being filmed, introduce her to her favorite stars, and make a big weekend out of it than give her earrings for Christmas. Both gifts may cost the same amount of money, but she has a lifetime memory with the former. Because they are all about being Chief Memory Makers, Paul and Steve's excitement for creating experiences spills over into their professional lives.

Hence, they enjoy creating experiences for their employees.

On one occasion they held a contest inside the headquarters and ended up taking a half dozen employees and some spouses to the Country Music Awards in Las Vegas, all expenses paid. There was even a special concert afterward with all kinds of celebrities in attendance.

At one point, Paul came into some awesome *Hamilton* tickets, two pairs in the pit orchestra, row four, the most gorgeous seats in the house. The musical was the hottest thing at the time, and the guys wanted to get everyone in the company involved in it. As with the $50,000 charity gift, Paul and Steve wrestled with how to make it fair. They did not have a lot of time because there was only a week and half before the event. So they created a raffle, Hamiltons for Hamilton. Because President Hamilton is on the $10 bill, the guys decided to sell $10 raffle tickets and let the employees pick the charity that would receive half the proceeds, while a local homeless shelter would receive the other half.

The two raffle jars each raised $500 for charity, and some happy employees won an experience of a lifetime. It didn't change anyone's life, but it made a social impact. And it reinforced a culture of compassion and fun.

GOOD CULTURE AND GOOD HUMOR

Before they go to HR that first day, every new hire spends the first hour meeting with Paul and Steve to hear their vision directly. The guys realize that new hires would be hearing a lot of things out on the floor, but they want new employees to hear from them first. And they always close the hour by asking the following question: "When you came in for your job interview, what was your experience with us?"

Most say something like, "It was overwhelming. People were coming up and making sure I was taken care of, asking if I needed anything. They went out of their way to introduce themselves."

To which the guys respond, "You've experienced firsthand our culture. Here's our challenge to you: help us perpetuate that culture because that's how important it is."

Paul and Steve talk about culture the very first day, the very first hour. And that's by design. They also create experiences for the staff, even at their own expense, literally and figuratively.

You might catch the guys walking through the building with a cooler on a hot day, handing out ice cream sandwiches like the Good Humor man. But it's in those playful, fun moments that the lifeblood of their organization is evident.

Culture is about creating a positive experience for your employees. Whether they've been with Paul and Steve for years or hours, the running joke is that now that they've worked for them, they are absolutely ruined. From that moment forward, they are never going to find another job, or a pair of bosses, who will love them like Paul and Steve do.

FRANCHISEE SPOTLIGHT:
KATY RIVERA

About Katy:

I am currently living in Tacoma, Washington. When I graduated from college with a degree in communications, my dream was to be on the radio. But what I was really good at was working with teenagers. After serving several years in my hometown of Sugar Land, Texas, I became a full-time missionary to the group of teenagers I loved the most, military teenagers. My parents were both military brats and I believe that is something that you carry with you your entire life. I moved to Belgium to work for the chaplain's office, where I was responsible for planning weekly, monthly, and yearly events for teens whose parents were serving across Europe. It was while I was in Europe that I met my husband, an active-duty soldier. When I got married, I began to move every one or two years and I was constantly changing jobs, but the one common thread was event planning. I found myself as an event coordinator at Borders, running fundraisers, and volunteering to plan events at every duty station. I am now a stay-at-home business owner and have two children, a seven-year-old daughter and a four-year-old son.

(From L-R) Jack Daly, Steve Davis, and Paul Trapp (Washington, DC—2007)

Steve Davis and Paul Trapp receive Inc. 500 award (Washington, DC—2013)

Early Steve Davis and Paul Trapp (Cocoa, FL—1993)

1LT Paul Trapp deployed to Hurricane Andrew (Homestead, FL—1992)

Steve Davis and Paul Trapp on vacation (Breckenridge, CO—2007)

Paul Trapp and Steve Davis at event (San Diego, CA—2007)

Early event staff with Kelly Perdew (San Diego, CA—2007)

*Paul Trapp, Cocoa Police Officer of the Year
(Cocoa, FL—1994)*

Steve Davis (Baghdad, Iraq—2003)

Steve Davis on dignitary protection detail (Baghdad, Iraq—2003)

President George W. Bush with Paul Trapp and Steve Davis (Crystal City, VA—2010)

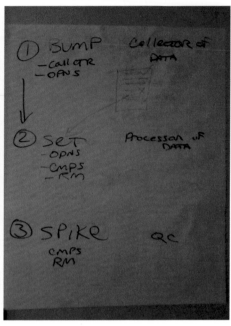

Coach Jason Horowitz and son Joshua (Hollywood, FL—2017)

Original flip chart used to describe bump, set spike to new employees (Dumfries, VA—2011)

Corporate charitable gifting event (Dumfries, VA—2013)

Federal Conference employees celebrating #23 on the 2012 Inc. 500 list w/ 23 gold coins each (Dumfries, VA—2012)

Combined Federal Conference and EventPrep holiday masquerade party (Washington, DC—2018)

Meet the Cast

Denise Radcliff... This top grossing box office star delivers an Oscar worthy performance as the "Bread Winner"...

Tina Mincks... portrays a low-key heroine with a performance that will leave you breathless... The Washington Post gave her Five Stars!

Femi Shodeinde... provides a brilliant performance that is sure to win him the Academy Award for Best Supporting Actor!

Jessica Davis... is a double Golden Globe Nominee for Best HR Director & Best Finance Director... She has truly earned her Star on the NCI Walk of Fame!

Kelly McWhinney... is an "A" Lister who is a force to be reckoned with! Her blockbuster performance will leave you sitting on the edge of your seat begging for more...

Dinner program insert to celebrate resiliency w/ five key leaders. Paul and Steve are forever indebted to this amazing team! (Washington, DC—2014)

Federal Conference employees celebrating #23 on the 2012 Inc. 500 list (Dumfries, VA—2012)

The birth of EventPrep, Inc. (Dumfries, VA—2016)

Pastor Garrick Pang and his wife, Anna, join EventPrep for a Franchise Discovery Day. Garrick and Anna are now EventPrep franchisees in Seattle, WA (Dumfries, VA—2018)

EventPrep trade show booth w/ franchisees (L-R) Michelle Mason, Alison Davis, and Danielle Marlar (Las Vegas, NV—2019)

(From L-R) Steve Davis, Reggie Aggaral, and Paul Trapp—Reggie is the founder of Cvent (the MLS of hospitality; Washington, DC—2015)

New franchisee Michelle Mason and her employee (Amy Elinski) join Paul, Steve, and Denise Radcliff (EventPrep executive vice president) at a midsummer concert (Bristow, VA—2018)

(From L-R) SPC Steve Davis, CPT Paul Trapp, SGT Jan Artley, and SPC Randy Jackson. Premobilization haircut for overseas deployment (Palm Coast, FL—1999)

This is a computer-generated sketch of Paul and Steve from a photo booth in a movie theater lobby. They crammed in the booth to take this picture about a month before they started Federal Conference, and it hangs prominently in Paul's office.

2LT Paul Trapp being sworn in by his friend and mentor LTC Bob Lewis (Camp Blanding, FL—1989)

Early days—IT director Femi Shodeinde working in Steve's basement on a makeshift desk made from computer boxes

Davis and Trapp families vacationing together (Breckenridge, CO—2007)

WO1 Steve Davis is commissioned as a warrant officer by his cousin Col. Billy Ketterer and MAJ Paul Trapp (Fort Rucker, AL—1989)

Special Agent Steve Davis from the Brevard County Drug Task Force teaches high school students about the consequences of illegal drug use (Camp Blanding, FL—1996)

Steve Davis and Paul Trapp with early Federal Conference staff at USMC event (Quantico, VA—2007)

Trapp family with Steve and daughter Maggie (Breckenridge, CO—2007)

Celebration of winning a new contract around the sacred Federal Conference Sales Bell (only rung when a sale is made). Employees gather with ceremonial noise makers to celebrate (Dumfries, VA—2013)

Executive Leadership Boating Retreat. (From L-R) Kimberly Trapp, Paul Trapp, Jessica Davis (EVP), Steve Davis, Keith Kruse (president), Leslie Kruse, Denise Radcliff (EVP), and Terry Redcliff (Occoquan, VA—2018)

Where did you hear about EventPrep?

I had just sat down to rewrite my résumé, trying to take nonprofit work and translate it into a "real job." When I looked at what I had done it came down to planning major events, fund-raising, and managing people. Less than a week after I decided to focus my career aspirations on event planning, a military spouse blogger said, "Hey, you should check out the giveaway these guys are doing." In the military you often hear of "giveaways" and kind of just think to yourself, "Yeah, okay," but as the process moved forward and I began to really talk to these guys, I started to think, *Maybe this is the real deal. So I went along for the ride to see where I would end up, and the next thing I knew I was a business owner.*

What motivated you to become a franchisee?

I want to feel as if I am building a strong foundation for my family. When you are married to a soldier, your life is at the will of the army. You go wherever they tell you, whenever they tell you. But your dreams and ambitions can sometimes fall to the background because you are trying to support a career without really having an opportunity to build your own. When I got married, I was a missionary, so I had a clear "calling" to serve, but I worked on a military contract. I could only work where a contract was, and if there wasn't a contract where we lived then I didn't have a job. So when I began to seek other opportunities, as soon as I was into the next round of interviews, we would get orders to move to a new duty station. It always felt as if I would have to wait until retirement before I actually got to begin my career. And I was educated, but not employable—no one wanted to hire someone they would only have for a year or two. After so many years picking up odd jobs, you often wonder when you will ever get the chance to build your own career. Paul and Steve dropped an opportunity of a lifetime into my lap. And they saw in me a potential that I knew I had, but was rarely recognized for.

The more I talked to Paul and Steve, the more I began to believe that they were the real deal, not just amazing salesmen. I was a tough sale, mainly because the world and everyone in it tells us not to believe that anyone is just going to give you something for nothing. Everyone I know was asking me, are you sure about these guys? I know that Paul and Steve believe in my ability and I also believe that they are going to help me to be successful. If I fail, it reflects on them also, and I do not believe they are going to let that happen. My brother-in-law has been in franchising for many, many years and when he read through our agreement he told me it was the real deal and no one was trying to get anything out of me. I believe in Paul and Steve, I believe in their vision, and I am proud to be a part of the team.

What were factors in your decision to become a franchisee?

Honestly, I didn't have a lot to lose. I had been seeking an opportunity that would allow me to contribute financially to my family and also build a career of my own, and this chance literally fell out of the sky. I am a quick learner and I know this is a business I can do, and I can do well. It was like someone said, "Okay, Katy, here is what you are good at, here is what you are looking for, here is an opportunity to grow something." How could I have said no? We are about to retire from the military, we are looking to buy our forever home, and I want to look at my children and tell them they can have whatever they need or want in life. And if I move, this goes with me!

How is your life today as a franchisee?

Life is fun. I love to be busy, meet new people, and learn new things. It is fun to give my husband the opportunity to be a full-time parent while I am away on business. It is fun to have new opportunities, to grow in new ways, to work at becoming a subject-matter expert in a new field. It is fun to have a new passion, to have a new topic of conversation as I get out and talk to people and show them how I can help them. I can now tell my daughter that she can be her own boss and that she doesn't have to let someone else be in charge. I can be home to play with my son, and still be writing contracts and talking to hotels.

What is the best part of being a franchisee?

The franchise model *works*. And you aren't alone. I have franchisees across the country that I am communicating with constantly. We are growing together. I own my own business, but I am still a part of a team. I am working with another franchisee to write our own playbook on client acquisition. Even though I am my own boss, I never feel as if I am left out on an island. There is a strong team of people working with me, cheering for me, and helping me to grow my business.

Chapter Seven

BEFRIENDING MURPHY

• • • • • • • • • • • • • • • • • • •

If plan A doesn't work, don't worry, you still have twenty-five letters left.

—ANONYMOUS

One hour before showtime, Paul and Steve's event planners were on-site and ready to deliver. Tina, Rachel, and Phil were extremely capable and talented, and had been working with the guys for nearly eight years by the time of that particular event. Tina, the lead, knew exactly how to respond under pressure and had dealt with just about every situation under the sun. The event was for a brand-new customer, so Tina and her team wanted to put their best foot forward to make a great first impression. Leading up to the event, they had done several dry runs, rehearsals of sorts, to make sure nothing went wrong.

The event was being held in a relatively remote area in the lower floors of the hotel. The Wi-Fi signal was weak, but even that wasn't an issue for Paul and Steve's seasoned team. They had brought along all the necessary technology for portable/enhanced Wi-Fi and tested it to make sure it worked properly. All of the equipment the team was using happened to be through a wireless provider that the guys had a relationship with for over a decade. The night before, the team did more dry runs and tested all the equipment again, and it looked like all was good.

With an 8:00 a.m. launch on the big day, the event planners sprang into action at 7:00 a.m., turning on all the equipment, just as they had the night prior during the dry run. This time, however, there was no signal. Tina checked the outlets and connections, but the power was fine. For some reason the network was down. Mind you, everything that was about to happen depended on a Wi-Fi signal: the slide show, the presentation, the video the client needed to download … even the registration was web-based. In today's world, an internet connection is the difference between an event being a success or a failure.

With sixty minutes until showtime and counting, Paul, who was in Florida at the time, got the call. Before long, the entire senior staff was alerted to an epic failure about to happen with a new customer. Murphy had arrived! Yet, like a duck gracefully gliding across a pond as smooth as glass while beneath the surface his little legs are going a thousand miles a minute, the event planners dealt calmly with the customer. Total game face. Nothing to see here, just checking the equipment.

The team at the headquarters in Virginia scrambled to make sense of the unexpected loss in internet service. A call with the cell phone carrier revealed the source of the chaos. Months earlier, Paul and Steve's company bank account had been compromised, so they had to shut everything down and get all new bank accounts and credit/debit cards. Evidently someone on the finance team had neglected to notify the cell carrier that the credit card on file, which was set up for autopay, was no longer valid. No payment equals an interruption in service.

As the guys worked to resolve and update the payment method on their end, the event planner at ground zero pulled out her personal cell phone with her hot spot and saved the day. A redundancy plan was in place, disaster was averted, and the client lived happily ever after, unaware of the potential threat to a successful meeting.

Murphy's Law—"Anything that can go wrong, will go wrong"—has never been truer than in the event planning business. In fact, with more than three thousand events each year, Paul and Steve have become so adept at dealing with Murphy that when he shows up at an event unexpectedly, as in the previous anecdote, they recognize him, welcome him, credential him, and provide an escort to show him around.

THE MANY FACES OF MURPHY

To deal with Murphy and the endless ways he might show up at any given event, Paul and Steve created an internal system similar to the mobilization books they used in the military, called in-process reviews (IPRs). In the weeks leading up to an event, the team would review every possible detail, meet with the client, and scope out the venue. Basically, they ran through every scenario, both likely and unlikely, in an effort to be prepared when Murphy showed up.

Back in the early 1990s when Paul's wife, Kimberly, worked as a 911 dispatcher, the internet was not available. On her desk sat a Rolodex, which contained note cards bound on a rotating wheel with quick responses to common emergencies listed alphabetically. When a distressed person would call to report a person choking on food, or a mother going into labor, Kimberly could flip through the Rolodex, find the corresponding card, and offer advice on what to do. Because Murphy is going to show up in any number of forms, when preparing to do anything, there has to be a list of solutions in place before a problem ever happens.

BECAUSE MURPHY IS GOING TO SHOW UP IN ANY NUMBER OF FORMS, WHEN PREPARING TO DO ANYTHING, THERE HAS TO BE A LIST OF SOLUTIONS IN PLACE BEFORE A PROBLEM EVER HAPPENS.

Part of Paul and Steve's preparation during the IPR for any given event is to brainstorm all the possible scenarios that could go wrong. What if the site loses power? Is there a backup generator? Who is in charge if the primary contact at the hotel has a medical emergency? What happens if one of the registration computers goes down? What if we run out of coffee during the break? If the client requires a general session with three breakout sessions in various conference rooms, that means every room needs a projector. So how many projectors do Paul and Steve bring? Five. They know better than to bring just four, because they need to have a backup projector in case Murphy shows up and breaks one at the exact moment when the client is sharing critical data with the audience.

Even the best event planner in the entire world can never—will never—be able to predict a fluke thing that goes wrong. But you're not necessarily planning for what could go right. You're planning for what could go wrong.

That means being prepared for literally anything.

As mentioned earlier in the book, event planners are among the top five most stressful jobs in the world. Paul and Steve should know ... they've made careers in three of the top five:

1. Enlisted military personnel—constantly risking one's life

2. Firefighter—having to run into burning buildings at a moment's notice ... and you thought that big project was really making you stressed!

3. Airline pilot—imagine the pressure of flying hundreds upon hundreds of souls around the globe every day.

4. Police officer—police officers are always under a great deal of stress and risk of life.

5. Event coordinator—they may not risk their lives or limbs, but they are still the people left holding the bag when anything—major or minor—goes wrong. If the hors d'oeuvres come out five minutes late—or early—or if the band has the wrong cord to connect their amp, or if there is a typo in the invitations ... you name it, they get yelled at. These aren't life-threatening stakes, but the stress is almost always high.

SWOT TEAM DEBRIEFING

Over the years, Paul and Steve have implemented a series of operations manuals and checklists. The ones executed during an event are of course critical to addressing Murphy whenever he decides to crash the party. But the checklist completed *after* the event is just as valuable a tool in predicting where Murphy might show up at the next event: the after-action review (AAR).

This tool gives the team a chance to measure the event's success by employing a SWOT analysis, a common review practice in business. An acronym for Strengths, Weaknesses, Opportunities, and Threats, SWOT is an invaluable tool for honestly evaluating and improving performance. The key word in that last sentence is honestly. Everyone involved in such an assessment needs to be as objective as possible when evaluating each category to ensure maximum results.

IDENTIFYING THE STRENGTHS AND OPPORTUNITIES OF AN EVENT ARE EASY. BUT EVEN MORE VALUABLE SOMETIMES ARE EXPOSING THE WEAKNESSES, BECAUSE WEAKNESSES PROVIDE AN OPPORTUNITY FOR IMPROVEMENT.

In fact, Paul and Steve are so serious about gaining insight into the execution of an event that they often include the client in the evaluation, asking their opinions, and even pointing out weaknesses the client never noticed. For example, something as simple as name badge distribution for the attendees can reveal a weakness. Do we preprint the badges? Do we print on-site? How many support staff should we bring to avoid a bottleneck at the registration counters?

If you've ever been to a conference, you're familiar with the table near registration containing dozens, if not hundreds, of alphabetized name badges all sprawled out. There's a tipping point in the number of attendees, however, where that's just not an efficient process. It gets too laborious and cumbersome, not to mention confusing, to have two thousand name badges on a table with attendees pawing through them. Once that tipping point is reached, it's much better to automate, similar to checking in and printing a boarding pass at an airport. The reality is, there's a formula for properly distributing name badges. Although industry standards recommend a 1:50 ratio of support staff to attendees, Paul and Steve opt for an increased ratio of 1:40 to ensure the highest level of customer care. Also, they will typically preprint name badges for events with up to three hundred attendees, but will recommend on-site/automated check-in/name badge printing for groups larger than that.

Identifying the strengths and opportunities of an event are easy. But even more valuable sometimes are exposing the weaknesses, because weaknesses provide an opportunity for improvement.

A CUSTOMER NAMED MURPHY

We're all familiar with the term *bridezilla*—a bride-to-be who is often considered demanding and demeaning, who instills terror in the hearts of wedding planners everywhere for her unreasonable requests and over-the-top emotional state. Event planners sometimes deal with such clients, those who inadvertently sabotage, or at least attempt to undermine, the whole process.

While a vast majority of Paul and Steve's clients trust them implicitly, turn it all over to them, and go off to bigger and better things, other clients can be the living embodiment of Murphy: high maintenance, needing to be on every call and know every detail, straying from the plan. Some get brilliant ideas at the last minute like, "Hey wouldn't it be cool if we just had the keynote speaker float down out of the rafters? Can you guys make that happen?"

It goes without saying that these clients are not intentionally trying to destroy the event. After all, it's their event, not Paul and Steve's. The client is the one on the hook for its success because it's five hundred of the client's closest business associates in the room. There's a lot of self-pressure for clients to look like rock stars. That's the main reason events can be so stressful: the client who *needs* to look good piles all that pressure onto the event planner to deliver.

So when the occasional customer is Murphy, there's a balance of accommodating patiently and making them look like the hero, never the villain. And letting them think it was *their* idea *not* to let the keynote speaker fly out of the ceiling.

MURPHY MAKES HOUSE CALLS

Being prepared for Murphy to show up is ingrained in Paul and Steve. They've brought that instinct to their careers in law enforcement and as police officers, and obviously later to event planning. In case you were wondering, even their personal lives are no exception. Just ask their families.

Paul's wife will often remind him that the opinion he is inserting in the conversation was never requested ... or needed. Prior to Thanksgiving break, his teenaged daughter was preparing to fly home from Virginia Commonwealth University for the holidays. He was doing checklists in his head. "Tell me, what your plan is for tomorrow?"

"I'm leaving my last class at 11:50 a.m. Then I'm gonna start packing," she said.

"Maybe you should pack tonight," Paul replied.

"Why should I pack tonight? I've got plenty of time tomorrow; my plane doesn't fly out until after dinner."

"Well, what you don't know is what's gonna happen tomorrow afternoon," he declared.

"But I was just gonna take a nap tonight, or just chill out."

Paul reluctantly conceded. "Okay. What time does your plane leave?"

"It goes wheels up at 7:30 p.m.," she replied.

"What time are you gonna leave your dorm?"

"I figure around 5:00 p.m."

"Okay, you're in Richmond, Virginia, in a college dorm. You're supposed to be at the airport two hours before your flight. Tomorrow is the busiest travel day of the year ..."

Clearly Paul lovingly protects his daughter from Murphy as best as possible. Steve is exactly the same way with his family. Needless to say, the guys even run through the same sort of routine with each other.

Once, when the two were heading out of town together, Steve began drilling Paul during the car ride to the airport. "Do you have your computer? Do you have your ID? Did you pack this ... did you pack that ... how about your wallet?" asked Steve, checking off his mental list.

The guys got to the airport, parked the car, and went to the kiosk to check in. Steve reached in his back pocket for his wallet ... which he had left at home.

Steve, of course, argues that he was left hanging as Paul never drilled him in return. But in the end their friendship survived. By the way, Steve was still able to board the plane without identification, because as a seasoned traveler, he had previously registered with CLEAR, which uses fingerprints and biometrics to identify travelers … again, preparation diverted a potential crisis.

INSTINCT TO PREPARE

Paul and Steve pride themselves on hiring people with that same instinct. Maybe the prospective employee chose the hospitality profession because she enjoyed the hotel setting. Maybe he went to college to get a degree in hospitality management, or received an event planning certificate, or simply relished planning events for friends and family as a hobby. Whatever the case, event planners have a desire to help customers enjoy an incredible experience. They love executing a successful event, then waking up and doing it again and again. Teaching that level of customer care, of dedication to the details, of selflessness and commitment to quality is difficult if not impossible.

So Paul and Steve see the preparation instinct built right into the DNA of their team, which ultimately defines the culture. Steve might find one of his people beating his or her head against the wall and ask what the problem is, only to find out Murphy has arrived and delayed the FedEx plane—the one with all the event name badges—on the tarmac. "Listen," Steve says, "I can't thank you enough. Because if it wasn't you suffering right now, it would be the client."

Steve knows all too well what it's like to step in the way of both literal and figurative bullets for another person. As a former special agent on a protection detail, Steve was required to step in between the principal he was protecting and the threat. His training and instinct kicked in, and he did it willingly.

For example, during Steve's deployment to Iraq in 2003–2004, he was responsible for protecting many US dignitaries in a combat zone where the threat level was extremely high. This selfless type of service translates well in regard to event planning as event planners often step between the client and the threat to shield them from the pain and embarrassment associated with a failed event.

That describes the nature of the event planners who work for Paul and Steve, and their level of commitment to the client. When (figurative) shots are fired, and the (figurative) bullets are flying overhead, they too instinctively step between the client and the threat to shield the client from the pain and embarrassment associated with a failed event.

And sometimes at the end of a particularly harrowing event, during the AAR, it becomes necessary to share with the client the disasters averted due to the planner's dedication to shield them while the sky was falling. The client is even more appreciative of the service provided and the opportunity to remain focused on their guests, and it reinforces their trust and reliance on Paul and Steve's team.

THE HUMANITY OF IT ALL

Of all the things that can undermine an event's success, chemistry wins the prize. Paul and Steve are prepared at all times to fix logistics, to streamline the process, and to address any hardware or software issues. But when clients pull them aside and say that they just don't click with the assigned event planner, it's another incarnation of Murphy entirely: personal chemistry.

It's maddening for the guys when they have someone who is a rock star event planner with a seven-year track record and not one complaint, but who just doesn't click with the client. Is it an analytical type trying to work with a salesperson? Is it a bubbly person rubbing a serious one the wrong way? These issues, too, are fixable, but they're extremely delicate because people's feelings and egos are attached to them.

To address this, Paul and Steve do their best to match the personality type of the event planner with that of the client. Paul and Steve use a series of assessment tools when hiring talent as part of their onboarding and ongoing training. The results aid them when playing matchmaker with new clients to ensure a successful outcome.

THE GREATEST COMPLIMENT

To illustrate how unpredictable Murphy can be, once in Philadelphia there was a bomb scare at the venue, right while the event was in full swing. Up until that moment, everything was going smoothly and flawlessly. And then suddenly a suspicious package was found at the hotel and everyone had to be evacuated.

PREPAREDNESS, RESOURCEFULNESS, AND HAVING THE GREAT RELATIONSHIPS PAUL AND STEVE HAVE WITH HOTELS AND VENDORS ALL OVER THE WORLD WILL WIN OUT OVER MURPHY EVERY TIME.

How do you possibly plan for that? You can't. Police flooded the area, the bomb squad arrived, and people were in panic mode. But the event planner automatically went into "save the day" mode. She was able to shift gears using Paul and Steve's industry relationships to place the attendees in an adjacent hotel so they could continue their meeting with minimal inconvenience. It was an expedient alternative that caused minor disruption, but the show must go on.

Preparedness, resourcefulness, and having the great relationships Paul and Steve have with hotels and vendors all over the world will win out over Murphy every time. Because of their purchasing power with the major hotel chains, and the relationships built between the event management team, the event planners, and the hotel personnel, the guys can get just about anything done at a moment's notice. When something is wrong with the food, the AV, or the room setup, they can rely on the experience of their team and their industry relationships to help resolve all of those problems on the ground, from Boise to Brooklyn, London to Okinawa.

And the best compliment Paul and Steve ever receive, which happens often, is when the client realizes the guys and their team are not just being responsive to their needs; they are being proactive. The client finally has a sense of confidence and says, "You know, by this time of day, while everyone else has gone out to dinner, I'm usually working until midnight trying to get things get ready for the next day. I'm actually going to go out to dinner with them because I feel really comfortable that you guys got this. I'll see you in the morning."

When a client can trust you with their baby, and can go out to dinner and enjoy themselves and visit with their associates like they deserve to, that says a lot.

FRANCHISEE SPOTLIGHT: ANGELA SPANGLER

About Angela:

I live in Fayetteville, North Carolina. I was born and raised in Akron, Ohio. After Jeffrey and I were married, we moved to Nashville, where he finished his senior year of college. I planned to finish my schooling one day after he wrapped up seminary school and became a pastor. As God would have it, we had our first baby while Jeff was at seminary in Kansas City, Missouri. I worked full time and our daughter went to daycare as Jeff worked and studied. Before long, we found ourselves in Florida on our second church assignment, expecting baby number two. I worked full time doing health insurance and daycare. Jeff joined the Army Chaplaincy, which is where God led us next. Twenty-two years, three more kids, and many moves later, we found God directing us to start thinking about the next chapter.

A friend of ours told me about EventPrep, and said he was praying about it as his possible next chapter. He told me about a military spouses franchise giveaway that they were doing. Since I had never finished college and thought all I had was my "professional volunteer" experience to offer, I reluctantly began the process. I sent in my essay but hadn't done step two. One day, Melissa called from EventPrep and asked if I was going to finish my entry. I told her all the reasons why I didn't think I had much to offer. She told me Paul and Steve were doing the giving away to honor their own wives by honoring spouses like me, spouses who had faithfully supported their soldiers through the years to allow them to serve our country!

So I completed the entry. Each time I made the cut, I told a few more people. I started to pray even harder for God to close the door of this opportunity if it was something that would hinder my marriage or family. The next step was a video interview and I was dreading it. I was helping a new spouse who was coming to town to house shop via Skype. I was finished going through the house and I got a phone call. It was Paul Trapp. I thought, What in the world is he calling me for? As we spoke, he just let me share my story and my heart, and after listening and talking for a good hour, I shared that my husband was planning to retire soon and start pastoring again. I would need to find a job at forty-eight without a college degree and "only" experience and service for my résumé. He encouraged me to make the video and reiterated that he and Steve were honoring their wives by giving to other supportive active-duty military spouses. He really inspired me to believe in myself, and said all the experience with retreats and events would serve me well in this business. He also said that the easy part would be to teach me the business, because he thought I had integrity, joy, and a kind sense about me—qualities that they were looking for, which can't really be taught.

With that new shot in the arm of confidence, I talked to the camera and watched myself say all I needed to say. Finally, my sweet brother Jason Lee (who was videoing me) told me to just look at him and tell my story. I grabbed my coffee cup (so I wouldn't wave my hands so much) and just told him my story and well ... with all the wonderful voting support of my friends and family, I won one of the five franchises! Nothing short of a miracle. A stay-at-home mom and professional volunteer, serving God by serving soldiers and families for more than two decades, won an event planning franchise.

Who knew that while Jeff was working hard on active duty and earning a second master's, followed by a doctorate of ministry, and while I was volunteering and giving to the army and local communities all those years, God was actually preparing me/us for this? Jeff is doing a wonderful job as senior pastor and executive board member for Fayetteville Urban Ministries. The kids are all doing great and are active members of society.

I am so proud to be their mom, the wife of a wonderful pastor, and I'm still volunteering and active in my church, seminary, and community, all while being a small business owner and operator with EventPrep, a company that truly lives by its motto: in business for yourself but not by yourself.

It has opened so many other opportunities for me to minister and help those in ministry. I am now a lay representative on the Nazarene Theological Seminary board of trustees. I'm actively working on training events for military, from singles to family events. I am scheduling and booking events for my denomination both here in North Carolina and all over the country. I am able to help them save both time and money so that they can use their time and money in more important areas.

I love the people I work with and I love getting to meet and talk to people from all over the country every day. What a wonderful country we live in! Truly, if you can dream it, you can achieve it! To God be the glory, great things He has done!

What is the best part of being a franchisee?

At EventPrep, the sky is the limit! There is an unlimited supply of support and encouragement when needed. It's professional, yet personal. It is truly something to be proud of and people you are honored to be associated with.

Chapter Eight

EMBRACING CHANGE

· ·

Difficulties break some men but make others.

—NELSON MANDELA

Every good business has a dark chapter … a time when it hits a big bump in the road.

This is Paul and Steve's dark chapter.

It was December 2013. Paul and Steve's event planning company, Federal Conference, was rolling along like nobody's business. The preceding year, it was number two on the Inc. 500 Fastest Growing Company in America list with $49 million in sales that year alone. They had no reason to believe that anything would change. The planning of their annual holiday party was well underway—invitations had gone out to fifty employees and their families, the band had been booked, and the Christmas bonuses were awarded the day before the party to get everyone primed and excited for the celebration.

By the way, when Paul and Steve celebrate with their employees, they go all out. The 2018 holiday party and bonus budget was over $100,000. They see the celebration as part of their culture. It's a time for everyone to acknowledge a job well done all year … and for the guys to say "thank you."

The Friday before the holiday party in 2013, Paul received an email from their federal government client, which at the time represented the majority of Federal Conference's business—nearly $40 million annually. The federal government had been shut down, which resulted in thousands of furloughed workers, and in turn caused the guys to lose their largest contract. To further compound matters, apparently many federal agencies had been making poor financial choices by throwing wild and lavish events that were embarrassing the federal government. In response, President Obama signed a cease and desist executive order for all government event planning. That didn't mean government employees and officials would stop meeting. It meant that all outside contracts ceased to exist until the government could sort the mess out and get a handle on excessive spending and waste.

As Steve and Paul prepared to pick up their tuxedos, their largest client informed them that they had two weeks to shut down the contract—a contract that encompassed most of Federal Conference's employees. The office at the time was abuzz with the spirit of the holiday season, laughter and humming in the hallways, people chatting about their dresses for the party, their hair appointments, their last-minute shopping.

Paul and Steve had to make a lot of decisions fast. The fact was everything was already in motion. The hotel contracts were signed, and deposits had been made. The guys considered scaling the entire event down to next to nothing to save as much money as possible, knowing they were essentially on the verge of going out of business and would need to lay off forty people in two weeks.

Paul and Steve decided to put on their game faces and push through. They would break the news to everyone on Monday, but wanted them to at least have a blissful last hurrah. It was one of the hardest things for the guys to do at that party, to socialize and spread cheer and wish them all a Merry Christmas knowing what was coming. Yet that is exactly what they did, and when Sunday rolled around, Paul and Steve called the senior leadership team together and broke the news.

The guys didn't know what they didn't know. They looked around at their employees having the time of their lives that evening and realized they had made a rookie business mistake: too many eggs in one basket. They had other contracts, but nothing as significant as the one they lost suddenly.

Every successful business has its dark chapter, and for Paul and Steve it had finally arrived.

THE BOMB SHELTER

The military conducts an exercise in which you pretend World War III has started and you're in charge of a bomb shelter. Via radio communications with the higher headquarters, they say they're sending you a dozen people to put in your bomb shelter, but it only holds seven. You have to look at each person and assess them and what they bring to the table and decide which seven get in and which five don't. Basically it's a leadership exercise that asks you to play God, because the seven survivors you choose may be the only humans left on the planet. They would be responsible for rebuilding and repopulating the globe.

Your decisions on who to save will define what the new world will look like. Every potential survivor comes with a positive and negative attribute, so you are forced to weigh your choices very carefully. For example, one of your options is a priest, the only religious person in the mix. If you want religion to survive, he's the only way. But he's also celibate, which limits reproduction possibilities.

It's a powerful exercise, and eerily echoed the one that Paul and Steve faced when they met with their senior leadership team. Literally 90 percent or more of their workforce needed to be cut, and they needed to decide who was essential to the survival of the business. To this day the guys admit it was the hardest thing they ever had to do as business owners, to look in the eyes of people who they considered family, the ones who had made them successful, the ones who had dreams.

As with everything else they do, Steve and Paul decided to do it with dignity. In the two weeks of transitioning their team members out of the company, the guys hosted job fairs in their training room. They brought in competitors that were hiring. They brought in the Department of Labor, and coaches who could teach their employees how to write résumés. And they paid for it all.

The way the guys saw it, the culture of their organization shouldn't stop because the money stopped. The culture was in their DNA. In the end they decided they had just enough money to keep five key employees on board, each with unique capabilities. Just like with the bomb shelter, those employees' talents would determine the future of Federal Conference.

Paul and Steve were the first to take massive pay cuts, and the other five were assured half their usual salary for the following three months. If the survivors couldn't make something happen in ninety days, the dream would be over and the doors to Federal Conference would close.

Femi, Jess, Denise, Kelly, and Tina all agreed to the terms and conditions. And they agreed to do it with no guarantee that things would change or how long it would take. They knew that they were going to have to work twice as hard for half the pay. There were back-stories to the guys' individual relationships with those five people. Deep, personal connections. From Steve delivering furniture and gardening equipment to their homes, to helping them with yardwork and construction, the guys consider those five people family.

Literally, Paul, Steve, and their core team lived quarter to quarter for that entire year.

RESILIENCE TO REBUILD

The pendulum had swung really hard, really fast toward failure, but slowly over the next twelve months it began to swing back, returning a semblance of normalcy. It was a full year later before the big government contract the guys had lost came back up for bid. Through sheer grit and determination they won it back, and by the end of the year Paul and Steve were able to reinstate those key five people back to their original salaries, with a bonus, and Federal Conference began growing again.

The next order of business was to circle back to the other employees who had been laid off and ask them to come back and join the team. Steve personally did every single bit of the hiring, and almost every employee who was unemployed at the time or not happy with their current job left and came back to Federal Conference.

When the dust settled and Paul, Steve, and the team emerged

from the bomb shelter, they went back to all of the lessons they had learned and decided to do things differently. They decided to diversify their business and explore the commercial market instead of relying on one government contract as their bread and butter. Their processes got better and stronger during those twelve months of hardship, and they realized no contract defined who they were. They had passion and skills that could never be taken away, and that thought was empowering.

UNBROKEN

As they approached the end of their darkest year, the theme for the 2014 holiday party was Unbroken, based on the movie of the same name about the survival of a US soldier and former Olympian who endured horrific conditions as a prisoner of war during World War II. Where Paul and Steve had always thrown massive parties at the end of the year with live bands and open bars, that year's version was humbler, more intimate.

The guys had a really nice, high-end dinner, but there wasn't a live band. They didn't have sixty people on the floor dancing and child care on site so the adults could have fun. It was different, yet somehow just as meaningful: five couples sitting around the table with the owners at a nice restaurant.

It was celebration enough that Federal Conference had survived. Like the movie, Paul, Steve, and those five dedicated individuals remained *unbroken*. They couldn't be defeated despite the circumstances that had befallen them. Inch by inch, they were able to crawl forward, without any goal other than survival.

The dinner program was done in the fashion of a playbill, and on the front was the movie's iconic scene of the lead character struggling to hold a four-by-four above his head. On the inside cover was this letter:

To Our Precious Employees and Families ...

2014 represents the most challenging year in the history of our company, and we stand here together today, only because of the sacrifices each of you and your families made on our behalf.

As we look back, we will always remember the lessons we learned together, and the resiliency that each of you so proudly demonstrated by enduring long hours, lighter paychecks, and limited resources. Forced to do more with less, and you did all of this with a smile on your face and without a single complaint.

You have truly earned a place of honor in our hearts, and we are forever grateful to each of you.

2014 is now coming to an end and will forever be referred to as "The Year of Resiliency"... But watch out 2015, because we're not finished yet, and we're only getting stronger!

With much love and appreciation,

Steve & Paul

That particular document is framed and matted, and hangs on the wall right between Steve's and Paul's offices. Even to this day, those five people remain the core of Federal Conference. The guys are truly indebted to them and often say if it wasn't for those five people, they would probably be employees somewhere else.

FAB FIVE SPOTLIGHT: DENISE RADCLIFF, EXECUTIVE VICE PRESIDENT, EVENTPREP

About Denise:

 I was born in Minnesota, but have lived in Virginia since 1979. My wonderful husband and I have been together almost twenty-five years. We have two happily married daughters and six rambunctious grandkids, ages one to nine. My husband and I are avid boaters who enjoy boating on the Potomac River. My passion for planning/organizing spills into my personal life as I volunteer my time as the rear commodore for the Potomac River Yacht Clubs Association (PRYCA) and presiding coordinator for the Occoquan River Maritime Association (ORMA). Both organizations promote fun and safe boating on the Potomac through a number of events throughout the summer.

How did you meet Paul and Steve?

In 2011, I had been working for a small company that sold spare parts for military aircraft and weapon systems. I did a little bit of everything for them (sales, marketing, office management, HR, etc.), but the part of my job I liked the most was coordinating and participating in international trade shows (London, Paris, Singapore, etc.). I had been with the company for twelve years and was ready for a change when I saw an ad for Federal Conference on Craigslist for someone to organize/manage/attend a series of domestic trade shows. I applied for the job, but never received a response. Almost three months later, Paul reached out and said that position had been filled, but they had another opportunity to discuss. Shortly thereafter, I interviewed with Steve to be a team manager for a group of event planners who would support the army contract. I was terrified to leave the security of my job, but Steve was convincing and after quite a few conversations, I decided to join the team. Due to the army's contractual demands, Federal Conference wanted me to start immediately, but out of respect for my previous employer, I wanted to give two weeks' notice. In an attempt to satisfy everyone, I made one of the worst decisions I've ever made in my professional career—I suggested that I work mornings with my previous employer and afternoons with Federal Conference. I thought this would be a good compromise that would make everyone happy. It was horrible. It was incredibly awkward leaving my previous employer every day at noon to go to my new employer. On the flip side, I would arrive at Federal Conference at 1:00 p.m. and everyone was already knee-deep in planning. I missed critical structural meetings in the morning and Paul and Steve basically excused me for the first two months I worked there.

It was a very bumpy start and for weeks, I wondered if I had made the right decision. We were building the company structure from ground zero and every day was a new challenge. Luckily for me, I was two offices away from Paul and he heard me on the phone solving client issues and working with our hotel partners to be sure they were happy. Slowly, he and Steve warmed up to me and began understanding my skill set and how I could best support Federal Conference. Like Paul and Steve, I am a builder. I am extremely organized, and I *love* spreadsheets and flowcharts. These assets allowed me to assist the team in building the foundation of our systems and processes that are still in use today.

In 2012, Paul asked if I would be interested in joining them on another venture. November 1, 2012, was my first official day as senior account executive for the newly formed commercial division called Davis-Trapp. My job was to create marketing materials, build the internal sales process, and cultivate relationships with potential clients. Over the next few years, I concentrated on building our sales base by winning the trust of potential clients, but that was the easy part. Our client retention rate was 95 percent, solely due to the hardworking operations team that delivered stellar service. Clients continue to recontract with us to this day because our ops team is passionate about planning great events and truly cares about supporting our clients.

In 2016, Paul confided in me that he had gone to a franchising trade show and was considering expanding our capabilities through franchising. Initially, I was not convinced it was a good concept, as I had very little knowledge of franchising and it had a negative connotation in my mind. Paul is ever the optimist and is a fantastic salesman. The more we talked about it, the more I began to see the vision. Paul, Steve, and I would discuss strategy and structure, big picture, and details for hours on end. The more research I did, the more I understood the value of the franchising business model and how we were perfectly poised at that moment to create a successful brand in the space. I have enjoyed using my previous experience to build systems and processes for EventPrep, but I've also enjoyed learning about franchising. Paul and Steve have invested thousands of dollars in me to ensure I'm learning as much as I can about the industry through conferences, networking events, and real-world experience. This hands-on process has been the education of a lifetime. I'm grateful for the opportunity to work with everyone along the way and I'm excited to see what the future has in store for us all!

Why did you decide to stick it out through the difficult times?

One word: trust. During down times, I trusted that we would do things differently and move forward one step at a time without continuing to make the same mistakes. I trusted in Paul and Steve's vision and leadership. I trusted that we could and would pull together as a team to rebuild what was broken. Likewise, Paul and Steve trusted me to put the interests of the company first and do whatever was needed to ensure client happiness. They trusted my judgment and if I made a wrong turn, they trusted that I would learn from it and do it differently next time. We have the same philosophy and beliefs when it comes to customer service, which makes it easy to trust their vision for EventPrep.

What is the best part of your job?

I *love* what I do. It's incredibly rewarding to watch someone learn about EventPrep and trust us enough to make the huge decision to change their life and become a franchisee. I love the camaraderie of my colleagues and that I can count on them for help if/when needed. I love the process of creating something, testing it, and tweaking it. I love that every day is new and different.

KELLY MCWHINNEY, CMP, DIRECTOR OF EVENT SERVICES, FEDERAL CONFERENCE

About Kelly:

I currently live near Southern Pines, North Carolina, with my husband and two wonderful little girls. I've been an event planner/director for sixteen years, eight of those with Paul and Steve.

How did you meet Paul and Steve?

I was working at a hotel in Washington, DC, and was introduced to them by a colleague.

What motivated you to join the company?

When I first came to work with Paul and Steve, I had spent eight years as an event manager at various luxury hotels. I was excited about the opportunity to work on "the other side" of the event planning world and experience another dimension of my career. Additionally, I'd always been interested in being part of a small business where I could grow personally and professionally, and Paul and Steve were kind enough to provide me with the opportunity to have a big impact in shaping the present and future of their company. Once you meet Paul and Steve, it's not hard to immediately want to be a part of their team ... they are captivating, inspiring, and motivating.

Since I met Paul and Steve, they have treated my family and me as their own family. They have always worked hard to build their business, but also to help their employees grow professionally and personally, and have never wavered from that philosophy. Over the past eight years, my life has changed drastically: my husband has deployed overseas on three occasions as a contractor for six-plus months, I've had two children, and my husband's job relocated us to another state. The support Paul and Steve provided during these life-changing events has been unwavering and served as a constant. I am truly blessed to have them in my life! One quality always stands out to me about the way they run their business: the customer *always* comes first. It truly doesn't matter what it takes or how it affects the bottom line. I have seen the sacrifices they have both made to keep our customers beyond satisfied. It's an honor to work for a company that encourages you to do the right thing each and every day. It speaks volumes about their character and integrity.

What helped you decide to stick it out through the difficult times?

Regardless of the situation, Paul and Steve have always shown me that they value my insight and what I bring to the company. I've always had input into our operations, direction, and future plans. We have experienced numerous ups and downs as a company over the years and it's comforting to know that they always have my back. They have taken great care of me during the good times and I felt like it was my turn to take care of them during the tough times.

How is your life today working with them?

I'm excited about continued growth and future opportunities. I've been able to raise my family and always maintain a great work-life balance. I am starting the transition from my current role at Federal Conference over to a new role with EventPrep. I'm honored and humbled that they are allowing me to be a part of their next adventure together.

What is the best part of your job?

I have always felt like my work matters, and that my input is valued. I've grown throughout this experience, and hope to continue to do so in the years to come.

Conclusion

BEYOND THE BOOK

• • • • • • • • • • • • • • • • • • • •

It's never too late to be who you might have been.

—GEORGE ELIOT

So here you are at the end. Yet the end of one thing only sparks the beginning of another. What lies ahead? Not for Paul and Steve, but for you. After all, this story may be about Paul and Steve, but beyond the book is your story. You have the power to write the next chapter of your life.

You've walked the journey with Paul and Steve throughout this book you're holding in your hands. Just like with every single thing that has happened to them, they had been preparing for the entire time. Whether you know it or not, what you have to realize is that you've been preparing your entire life for this very moment. Every job, every setback, every time you've fallen and gotten back up, every experience has led to you reading these very words at this moment in your life.

Whether you become one of their employees or buy a franchise, or just go off and do your own thing, Paul and Steve want you to achieve your dreams. You are reading this book for a reason. In reference to the quote above, Paul and Steve didn't want to live with regret. They didn't want to look back at who they might have been, but who they were destined to become.

And if you think you are too old, or too young, or too broke, or not smart enough, or not organized enough to succeed, you are wrong.

Paul was just a few months shy of his fiftieth birthday when he started his first business. Not only that, but he had recently filed for bankruptcy due to the housing crash in the mid-2000s. Like millions of US homeowners and businesses at that time, he had zero money. That was one of the most defeating feelings he had ever experienced in his life. But he restructured his debt and kept focused on the road ahead. At the time of this writing, a little over ten years later, Paul and Steve's business had reached $51 million in annual sales.

If you are reading this book, chances are that you stand at a crossroads in your life. And whether it's joining Paul and Steve on an adventure or a totally different path, the fact is that you're searching for something. The question is: Do you want to continue doing what you're doing currently? If you do, put the book down—you're done. If this book has helped you think some things through and you decide you want to stick with plan A, which was go to college, get a good job, build a retirement fund … then good for you. That's how 90 percent of America works. We need you out there doing that. Thank you for reading.

But if you're still thinking that there is something more for you, if this book opened your eyes to a different way of thinking, then you have a choice to make. All of the skills that you've acquired, all the bullet points on your résumé, all of the past employers who will say nice things about you, when you left those relationships, when you left college, when you left your last job, when you left your last girlfriend or boyfriend, whatever it was you left, you took with you a new set of skills and experiences that are yours to keep. All of that is the preparation, your life's preparation for this moment. So what are the next steps for you?

Pick up the phone, give Paul and Steve a call, or visit their website *(www.EventPrepFranchise.com)*. They are genuinely, sincerely interested in you, and helping you succeed. Remember the advice Major General Ronald O. Harrison gave to Paul: "Go find young people of promise and enable them to become."

That's what Paul and Steve do for a living. They help people Prep for Success … so they can achieve their dreams.

So they can become.

ABOUT THE AUTHORS
• • • • • • • • • • • • • • •

Paul Trapp and Stephen Davis are lifelong friends who met over thirty years ago when Paul was on his way to attend Catholic seminary. They were the best men in each other's weddings, were godfathers to each other's children, and carried each other's parents to their final resting place. Their professional lives are also closely intertwined, as they've served together as law enforcement officers, deployed together as military officers, and been successful business partners for over three decades. You could say they are brothers by choice.

After several false starts, Paul and Stephen launched their first successful business in February of 2006, which is called Federal Conference, Inc. (Federal Conference was a bootstrapped startup providing professional event planning and management services to the government and commercial marketplaces and is currently based out of Northern Virginia.)

Federal Conference enjoyed moderate growth during its infancy, but experienced explosive growth during their adolescent years, becoming a two-time Inc. 500 award recipient: number twenty-three on the 2012 list and number two on the 2013 list, with $49 million in annual sales and 24,830 percent growth over the preceding three years. During that time, Federal Conference was also named to the Best Places to Work in the Industry List by *Meetings and Conventions* magazine.

Federal Conference now enjoys its status as a mature company and currently plans and executes over three thousand events annually across the globe, generating annual revenues north of fifty million pretax dollars.

STEVE DAVIS & PAUL TRAPP

In 2016, Paul and Stephen recognized they wanted to continue growing their business, but didn't want to take on more employees or overhead. After much brainstorming and discussion, they decided to hire their backfills and move their families back to Florida to start a new business venture that focused on growth in the commercial markets.

Franchising was the answer! Becoming franchisors would allow for rapid growth without the associated costs. Paul and Stephen packaged up all the lessons they learned, proven systems and processes, and their proprietary event management technology platform and launched EventPrep, Inc. As emerging franchisors, they now sell home-based franchise opportunities that specialize in event planning and management services. Entrepreneurial-minded hospitality professionals could now own a lifestyle business, working for themselves, but not by themselves.

EventPrep, Inc. currently supports sixteen franchisees throughout Arizona, Colorado, Florida, Georgia, Illinois, Kentucky, Maryland, New York, North Carolina, Texas, Virginia, and Washington State.

Paul Trapp—Paul is a founding owner and currently serves as the CEO of EventPrep, Inc. He is a former senior military leader who served as chief of recruiting for the Army National Guard and successfully managed a national sales force of over 4,500 military recruiting personnel. Paul started his recruiting career as a production recruiter and quickly achieved Master Badge status; he also worked in several recruiting leadership positions before he moved to National Guard Bureau Headquarters and expanded his sales influence to include a national reach. He also served as principal adviser to all family and quality of life issues and programs throughout the fifty-four states and territories. He holds over thirty years of experience in contract management; event planning; and organizing and evaluating conferences, seminars, and meetings in both the private and federal sectors.

Stephen Davis—Steve is a founding owner and currently serves as the president and COO of EventPrep, Inc. He is an accomplished, results-oriented, multistate operations director, with proven abilities in conference development, implementation, management, and conference design. Steve has experience in numerous state-wide conference implementation start-ups (e.g. conferences, workshops, training events, and third-party site selection). He motivates others toward achieving corporate, operational, and strategic goals through application of sound management principles. Steve is committed to ensuring superior customer service and public relations while assisting the further growth of the corporation. He provides direction and guidance throughout the company, underscoring the need to meet corporate philosophy, company goals, and objectives. He currently serves as a chief warrant officer and CID special agent in the Army Reserves. Steve deployed twice in support of the Global War on Terrorism.

OUR SERVICES

EVENTPREP

EventPrep is a forward-thinking, full-service event planning and management company with our corporate headquarters located in Central Florida. Our reach is global and our primary focus is to save our clients time, money, and anxiety while planning unforgettable events. We view ourselves as partners with our customers, our employees, our community, and our environment. We are a globally recognized brand name, capitalizing on our in-depth industry experience and leveraging our industry relationships. Our mission is moderate growth, annual profitability, and maintaining a sense of humor.

EventPrep makes the business of event planning and management streamlined, simple, and efficient for the client. The EventPrep franchise is designed to replicate our proven business model into new markets with professionals who exemplify the same motivation to serve and the willingness to go the extra mile for the client. We offer you the systems, support, and business model; you bring the willingness to learn, execute, and build.

We are a company founded by veterans, and our company philosophies, work ethic, integrity, and commitment to service are derived from our time in uniform. We can't express enough gratitude and thanks to others who have served our great country and the families that support them. Make the call today, get the discussion started, and see how we can help you build a future for yourself and your family.

To learn more how you can be in business for yourself, but not by yourself with an EventPrep franchise, visit **www.EventPrepFranchise.com.**

To learn more about our event planning and management services, visit **www.eventprep.com.**

EVENTPREP FRANCHISE

- **Twitter**: https://twitter.com/eventprepfran
- **Facebook**: https://www.facebook.com/EventPrepFranchise/
- **LinkedIn:** https://www.linkedin.com/company/eventprep-franchise-inc/
- **YouTube**: https://www.youtube.com/channel/UCx72Vy2BJdKr4aR8GLdR48A

EVENTPREP, INC.

- **Twitter:** https://twitter.com/myEventPrep
- **Facebook:** https://www.facebook.com/EventPrep/
- **LinkedIn:** https://www.linkedin.com/company/eventprep
- **YouTube:** https://www.youtube.com/channel/UC3kZ3sj5HNWL1Zmxb8SMV3A

FEDERAL CONFERENCE, INC.

Federal Conference is a forward-thinking, full-service event management company. Since 2006, we have successfully planned and delivered more than fifteen thousand meetings, conferences, and trade shows worldwide for associations and commercial and government customers. Our planning team is industry certified and experienced in creating innovative event programs that increase attendance, maximize revenue, and deliver an exceptional experience for all event participants.

At Federal Conference, *our expertise is your event.* Our expert planning team works closely with our customers to alleviate the burden of chasing numerous logistical details, allowing them to focus on what they know best: the content and vision for their event. We develop a management plan that is custom to our customers' specific requirements. We leverage best-in-class solutions for event plan, site selection, registration, housing management, and on-site event delivery to make every event extraordinary and stress-free. We specialize in the following:

- Event and Conference Planning
- Program Management
- Technology Solutions
- Facilities Management
- Marketing Services
- Speaker Management
- Conferences and Conventions
- Trade Shows and Expos
- Annual Meetings

- Board Meetings

- Corporate Meetings

- Sales Meetings and Product Launches

- Team Training

- Social Meetings and Retreats

FEDERAL CONFERENCE, INC.

- **Twitter:** https://twitter.com/FederalConf

- **Facebook:** https://www.facebook.com/
FederalConference/

- **LinkedIn:** https://www.linkedin.com/company/
federalconference

- **YouTube:** https://www.youtube.com/channel/
UCjDrFAOO5o_Ltdl8i7awu9g